Zionism

SUNY series in Jewish Philosophy
Kenneth Seeskin, editor

Zionism

Past and Present

Nathan Rotenstreich

Foreword by
Ephrat Balberg-Rotenstreich

With an additional essay by
Avi Bareli and
Yossef Gorny

Afterword by
Shlomo Avineri

State University of New York Press

Published by
State University of New York Press, Albany

© 2007 State University of New York

All rights reserved

Printed in the United States of America

No part of this book may be used or reproduced in any manner whatsoever without written permission. No part of this book may be stored in a retrieval system or transmitted in any form or by any means including electronic, electrostatic, magnetic tape, mechanical, photocopying, recording, or otherwise without the prior permission in writing of the publisher.

For information, contact State University of New York Press, Albany, NY
www.sunypress.edu

Production by Diane Ganeles
Marketing by Michael Campochiaro

Library of Congress Cataloging-in-Publication Data

Rotenstreich, Nathan, 1914–1993
Zionism : past and present / Nathan Rotenstreich.
p. cm. — (SUNY series in Jewish philosophy)
Includes bibliographical references and index.
ISBN-13: 978-0-7914-7175-3 (hardcover : alk. paper)
ISBN-13: 978-0-7914-7176-0 (pbk. : alk. paper)
1. Zionism. 2. Israel. I. Title.

DS149.R643 2007
320.54095694—dc22 2006032532

10 9 8 7 6 5 4 3 2 1

Contents

Foreword vii

An "Inside Intellectual": Remarks on the Public Thought of Nathan Rotenstreich 1
Avi Bareli and Yossef Gorny

Chapter One Return and Modernity 47

Chapter Two Activity and the Present 61

Chapter Three Aspects of Renaissance 73

Chapter Four The Negation of the Diaspora 87

Chapter Five The Values of Israeli Society 101

Chapter Six Toward a Reformulation of Zionist Ideology 115

Afterword 127
Shlomo Avineri

Nathan Rotenstreich on Issues Relating to the Holocaust 133

Appendix 135
Ephrat Balberg-Rotenstreich

The Individual and Personal Responsibility 137

The Holocaust as a Unique Historical Event 155

Index 165

Foreword

The present book was written by my father, Nathan Rotenstreich, in the late 1980s and early 1990s. The manuscript was left in his literary estate, and the Rotenstreich Foundation, established for taking care of the vast literary estate he left behind, was engaged in the effort of bringing it to press. Most of this literary estate has been published in his lifetime, from the early 1930s and during the many years of his academic and public career.

This manuscript, titled by him *Zionism: Past and Present*, can be regarded as a kind of spiritual and intellectual legacy regarding a subject about which he wrote extensively. The publication of the book is an opportunity to thank all those who made it possible: Eli Eyal, chairman of the Rotenstreich Foundation, for his continuous dedication, support and friendship; Shlomo Avineri for writing the afterword, and together with Berel Lang for paving the way and supporting the publication of the book; Kenneth Seeskin for his patience and support as an editor; Avi Bareli and Yossef Gorny for writing the introductory essay; David Heyd and Dan Laor for their efforts at the Rotenstreich Foundation. And last but not least—the production team at SUNY Press—James Peltz, Diane Ganeles, and all those who took part in this endeavor and brought it to completion.

Publishing a book without the author to consult with and see to all the finest details is almost impossible. Without the help of all these people it could never have happened.

Ephrat Balberg-Rotenstreich

An "Inside Intellectual": Remarks on the Public Thought of Nathan Rotenstreich

Avi Bareli and Yossef Gorny

The essence of Nathan Rotenstreich's career may be adduced from an incident that took place in his early adulthood. In 1932, at the age of eighteen, he moved to Palestine. Rotenstreich was a member of the Socialist-Zionist youth movement Gordonia—a member of one of the first groups in the movement—and a faithful adherent of the halutsic (Zionist pioneering) ideology that the movement encouraged. In the natural course of events, he would have become a *haluts* (pioneer) along with the rest of the group. However, according to retellings by friends and family members, the leaders of the movement decided to treat him as an exception and have him enroll at the Hebrew University of Jerusalem. This, they thought, would allow him to make a more meaningful contribution to the nation.

Thus, Rotenstreich's endeavors in scholarship and research were from their outset pregnant with social and national significance and set within a political context. Rotenstreich was committed to the Jewish settler society in Palestine and the Jewish people and was their self-styled emissary. Furthermore, there was a public that did consider him its emissary and designate him to serve the causes of the collective. For decades, he was a member of the leading party in the Zionist Labor Movement, Mapai,[1] and enjoyed an easy proximity to its leaders, including David Ben-Gurion; he was also a key figure in a political group called Min ha-Yesod, a faction that seceded from Mapai in the early 1960s.[2] He maintained strong relations with Gordonia members in the kibbutz movement, in Mapai, and, later on, in Min ha-Yesod, and with their leader, Pinchas Lavon, a leading figure in Mapai who became the leader of Min ha-Yesod. Nevertheless, Rotenstreich was a strongly independent-minded intellectual who did not subordinate himself to anyone. He was *engage'*, devoted to the interests of the Jewish people at large, but did not submit his own judgment to any authority. His formative environment and national and social affiliations underlay his evolution into an "inside intellectual" who contemplated his society from the standpoint of one who was immersed in its life and who identified with it—in a critical spirit.

Nathan Rotenstreich was born on March 31, 1914, in Sambor, eastern Poland (today in Ukraine). His father, Dr. Ephraim Fischel Rotenstreich, was a Polish Zionist leader and an important public figure in his hometown. When independent Poland was founded in 1918, the elder Rotenstreich was elected to the Polish Senate and the Sejm as a representative of the General Zionist Party. The family moved to Lvov, where Nathan Rotenstreich finished high school. His teachers at the Hebrew University included Samuel (Shmuel) Hugo Bergman, Gershom Scholem, Julius Guttman, Leon (Haim Yehuda) Roth, and Joseph Klausner. In 1938, he completed his PhD dissertation on Marx's Theory of Substance. He worked with the Jewish Agency from the time he moved to Palestine until 1949, and in 1950 he became a senior lecturer at the Hebrew University.

Rotenstreich was one of the leading figures in Israeli academia in the country's formative years. His status was reflected in the official posts that he held: Dean of the Faculty of the Humanities at the Hebrew University (1958–1962) and rector of the University (1965–1969). After his retirement, he was vice-president of the Israel Academy of the Sciences and Humanities from 1986 until his death (October 11, 1993). However, Rotenstreich was also one of the leading exponents of academia and a personality of vast formal and informal influence in the affairs of Israel's universities. He was among the founders of the Israel Academy of the Sciences and Humanities (1963) and the enunciators of its basic principles; he was also the first chair of the Planning and Grants Committee (PGC) of the Council of Higher Education (1973–1979), a powerful institution that regulates the budgeting of Israeli universities and research institutes. Rotenstreich played an important official role in establishing the autonomy of research and higher-schooling institutes by shaping the modus operandi of the PGC. His political and organizational connections with the Zionist Labor Movement, the dominant force in Israel's first decades, did not diminish his commitment to academic autonomy. Rotenstreich was one of the academic leaders who buttressed the autonomy of Israel's universities and research institutions, assuring them a substantial degree of independence from the authorities. As he went about this, he also steered them toward identification with Israel's goals and national and social values.

Rotenstreich was noted as a philosophical commentator of world repute. Among other things, he was a leading personality at the Institute International de Philsophie in Paris and the Center for the Study of Democratic Institutions in Santa Barbara, California. His many works (more than 80 books and 600 philosophical articles in important journals) include profound and original interpretations of the philosophies of Kant, Hegel, and Marx, as well as discussions of additional and diverse issues in philosophy. In conjunction with his teacher, Bergman, he translated into Hebrew Kant's three *Critiques* and *Perpetual Peace*, and without a collaborator he translated Kant's *Religion within the Boundaries of Mere Reason*. By so doing, he made an important contribution to Israel's society and language that the country's academic philosophers rarely matched. This considerable effort reflected Rotenstreich's sociocultural commitment, which was also manifested in his continual research into Jewish philosophy and the encounter of Jewish thought—secular and religious—with the crisis of modernity. By exploring philosophical questions about the status of Judaism in the modern era, Rotenstreich sought to tackle the spiritual agonies of his national collective, modern Jewry.

It was this commitment that prompted Rotenstreich to reveal his public thought in journals and newspapers. Rotenstreich was one of Israel's outstanding publicists in the early decades and an important ideologue in the circles of Mapai and the Zionist Movement at that time. He published his writings in periodicals affiliated with Mapai and the Zionist Labor Movement, such as *Davar*, *Molad*, *Ha-po'el ha-Tsa'ir*, and *Min ha-Yesod*; in the newspapers *Ha'aretz* and *Ma'ariv*; and in many other forums. Our discussion will focus mainly on several aspects of his copious public writing but it will try to probe the philosophical origins of this writing as well. Since Rotenstreich was a Socialist Zionist in terms of ideological worldview and political and organizational affiliations, his thinking was typified by a visible synthesis of national and social outlooks—a synthesis based on striving for voluntary shaping of collective life at all levels. Zionism and Socialism merged in his thinking; one should not construe these two elements in his thinking as distinct and unrelated. Both stem from the same source: the striving for collective self-determination, and therefore are intrinsically connected in Rotenstreich's view. Although we mention the Socialist aspect of his critique of the sociopolitical shaping of the State of Israel in its initial years and note the same aspect in Rotenstreich's general views, we focus on his national outlook and his critique of the coalescence of Israel–Diaspora relations, since these are the main concerns of this book. We hope our remarks will help the reader of the articles in this book. Rotenstreich gathered the articles at the very end of his life and one may consider them his public testament.

The Voluntaristic Fundamental in Rotenstreich's Thinking

Nathan Rotenstreich's Zionist and Socialist worldview was pronouncedly voluntaristic. His thinking aspires to a life shaped by rational will rather than to succumb to what seems to be social and national realities. He was acutely aware of the yawning gap between human reality and people's aspirations; he also realized that any fulfillment of aspirations involves the negation of what is unfulfilled. This awareness steered him toward pointed diagnosis of the historical reality; that is, toward Realism. However, he did not limit himself to Realistic diagnoses and the exposure of the dialectic nature of fulfillment. Instead, he repeatedly urged his readers to take a straightforward view of reality in order to fulfill the will of the individual and the collective in reality.

In this respect, Rotenstreich was plainly a left-wing thinker in the original sense of the term "Left." He demanded that the individual and the collective transcend the social and national reality and shape it in their spirit, instead of succumbing to it and accepting it as given. Rotenstreich's voluntaristic intent may be traced to two important sources: Kantian ethics, which stresses the centrality of will guided by the imperatives of reason; and the Socialist Zionist halutsic movement, which is noted for idealism infused with the ardent will of free-spirited people who pledge much of their lives to service of the Zionist "general will" in Israel. Gordonia, Rotenstreich's youth movement, was one of the most important branches of this movement, and his interpretation of Immanuel Kant's philosophy was one of the mainstays of his own research. Evidently, however, Rotenstreich was committed above all to the voluntaristic outlook, which emphasizes the centrality of rational will, and it was this commitment that underlay his continual recourse, throughout his adult life and in his philosophical and public writings, to Kantian ethics and the values and hopes of the Zionist Labor Movement.

It is the strong convergence of political views and philosophical leanings in Rotenstreich that make him an "inside intellectual." We use this term to denote Rotenstreich's oscillation between being an intellectual, that is, a contemplator who, as such, maintains a distance from the reality of his object of contemplation, and his moral commitment to the shaping of this reality. The moral commitment at issue flows from his own philosophical contemplation, among other things, but also leads him "inward" and urges him to be involved, to manifest his Jewish affiliation intensively, and to take part in activities of political and social organizations of the Zionist Left that aspire to shape national and social patterns.

This convergence of Kantianism, Zionism, and Socialism around the focal point of rational will, if one may express it in shorthand, was conspicuous in Rotenstreich's public writing. The focal point of this convergence is visible in a lengthy series of articles that Rotenstreich published about Zionist and social issues. A salient and illuminating example—one of many—occurs in his article "Socialism and the Problem of Responsibility," published in late 1952 in the journal *Molad*. Rotenstreich's discussion of the concept of "responsibility" in the article is an applied development of two central concepts in the Kantian ethics of reason, "duty" and "autonomy." Rotenstreich bases the application on his interpretative view of Kant's theory of morality as essentially a philosophy of emancipation.

Rotenstreich's arguments in the article indicate that Rotenstreich's voluntarism and negation of determinism, on the one hand, and his Socialist outlook on the other are linked by the concepts of Kantian ethics. From Rotenstreich's standpoint, the question of responsibility of the individual who makes a moral decision and does not slide passively into a state of action pertains directly to the historical enterprise of the humanistic Left. It directly affects the fate of the socioeconomic enterprise of the left, which may be defined—especially by Kantian Socialists such as Rotenstreich—as a quest for authentic social existence arising from negation of the supremacy of the economic consideration.

"Socialism finds itself in a situation where it sees no other way of attaining the desired level of production than to behave as though it were not Socialism, and to nurture in the individual the urges of possession and of economic and social progress," Rotenstreich states at the outset of his argument in the article. The socioeconomic arrangements that Socialism has ordained, however, restrain these urges. Thus, the individual tumbles into a difficult zone that lies between encouraging these urges and restraining them. He "sees himself functioning as a capitalist and is judged as a Socialist. The beginning of his behavior should be capitalistic and its denouement should be . . . Socialistic."

This untenable and severely pernicious confusion occurs because Socialism separates its means from its ends. By so doing,

Rotenstreich believes, Socialism does itself a disservice. Socialism should not reduce itself to the anonymous regulatory frameworks of the welfare and planning state in order to alleviate slightly the inherent injustice of rationalism or economic efficiency, while individuals' actual behaviors continue to be guided by the profit motive even under Socialist dominion and regulation. By behaving thus, Socialism merely concedes its own defeat, because its main object since the time it was devised is the praxis in individuals' lives.

The flaw, in Rotenstreich's opinion as expressed in the article, is rooted in Socialism's perception of Man: "[Socialism] did not elevate the idea of responsibility to the rank of a central idea . . . ." Here Rotenstreich, champion of the idea of responsibility, proposes a Kantian amendment to the accepted Socialist theory of the time. In his opinion, man's demand for rights in its Socialist version, and *a fortiori* in its Liberal version, will inevitably metamorphose into hedonism and, in turn, to a stance made up solely of a demand from society. Rotenstreich preached something altogether different: encouragement of recognition of the individual's responsibility to his/her locality, a focus on the commonality of the individual and his/her personal and social activity. Such a focus, he hoped, might lead to an authentic or noninstrumental relationship between the individual and his/her actions. No longer would the action be perceived as a means but as "an objective and overt quasi-extension of his psycho-physical personality." Thus, of course, Rotenstreich regretted that the kernels of authenticity that had evolved in the Zionist Labor Movement were now, in Israel's first years, "awash in the whirlpool of the all-sweeping economic consideration."

Socialism expresses in nationalization a macroscopic view of society: it entrusts ownership to society in the macroscopic sense of the term "society." According to Rotenstreich, however, "Society did not appear in its concrete forms. . . . Whenever a society is anonymous, it appears as an organization and not as a concrete unit of life." Such a society encourages a culture of entitlement and leaves no room for the relationship of responsibility that intimacy presumes. Such intimacy is possible only where there is "an identity of economy and society" based on the idea of the kibbutz (the Zionist and Israeli commune), an idea regarding "a society in which economic activity is one of the manifestations of social action." Such an identity does not exist in all of the organs of the Zionist Labor Movement. An identity of economy and society can exist only in the kibbutz movement. But without such identity in some of its organs, the whole Zionist Labor Movement cannot be true to itself. Thus, "The fate of the Labor Movement depends on reinvigorating the kibbutz movement."

Rotenstreich's discussion of the concept of responsibility carries an implicit demand: the political, social, and economic institutionalization that the Zionist Left will shape during a specific formation-and-formalization period must leave room for personal autonomy. The individuals in the society he envisioned will be integrally related to, and interwoven in, the social and economic systems. Thus, the systems will be truly "theirs." The concept that inspired Rotenstreich's thinking here is authenticity, and therefore, as we have seen, he linked the demand for personal autonomy, or personal responsibility for one's life, with intimate social relationships that are difficult to apply to broad political systems. The difficulty that arises here recurs in Rotenstreich's extensive public writings. His conclusions often rest on profound critical analyses but express an untenable moralizing attitude when they encounter political reality. Sometimes they disserve his cause; they may, for example, encourage disengagement from the arena of concrete politics—which, after all, cannot be an arena of authentic individual expression. This would leave the political arena to visionless politicians.

Rotenstreich did not desire such an outcome, of course. He considered his intent decidedly political and regarded its crux as political institutionalization by means of the kibbutz movement, through the agency of collective socioeconomic circles that would be small enough to maintain individuals' responsibility for their society. He hoped that the kibbutz movement would continue to be a pioneering, society-serving elite, as it had been in the pre-independence period, and that it would now function as a paragon for society at large and would inspire society to emulate it.

Rotenstreich's voluntaristic if not Utopian inclination was strongly manifested in this article. In 1952, as mass immigration doubled Israel's population and forced the country to tackle issues such as how to feed its citizens, Rotenstreich urged his comrades in the movement, leaders of the new state, not to succumb to "the grim facts of economic reality." Reality has its own intrinsic force irrespective of the Socialist Zionists' willingness or unwillingness to succumb to it, he argued, whereas their existential logic required them not to succumb. In other words, society-building should not wait until the economic and global basis for a Socialist society could take shape. From his standpoint, the very act of waiting was tantamount to succumbing. Socialism must not postpone "the creation of a social cell of human significance at the present time," since in the absence of such a cell, "Socialism would create with its own hands a social organization that would render it void." Rotenstreich even claimed that rejecting the primacy of the economic consideration is essential for Israeli society specifically. Israeli society, he said, is struggling to establish the physical basis of its very existence, and the struggle may lead to a confusion of standards and the evolution of a unilateral "functionalistic consciousness." To forestall such a possibility, a renewal of the "consciousness of responsibility" and "the social cells that carry its imprint" is needed.[3]

Rotenstreich extended his fundamentally voluntaristic approach to his Zionist views. Active individuals, he said, are as responsible for the fate of their nation as for the shaping of their society. Zionism signifies the reappearance of the collective Jewish will in history, and the fulfillment of Zionism depends on the determination of individual members of the Zionist pioneering movement to pledge themselves to the cause of the Jewish people at large. Rotenstreich termed Zionism an autoemancipation movement, not only to follow Leon Pinsker's lead but also to stress its being a *voluntary* autoemancipation movement and Israel's nature as a sovereign political society composed of Jews, as opposed to the Emancipation in Europe and, in particular, in America, and the total latitude of American Jews, which are the consequences not of voluntary, autonomous acts by Jews but rather of circumstances independent of them.[4]

Israel's essence as a manifestation of the Jewish collective will in history served Rotenstreich as a basis for what he called "the primacy of the State of Israel" in Jewish national affairs and from the Jewish point of view. Israel is the result of a deliberate effort by Jews and, as such, is materially different from Jewish existence in Diaspora. Israel is the product of a deliberate *ab initio* decision by the Jews, as opposed to an *ex post* reality such as the Diaspora, which exists by mere force of facts. Therefore, Israel deserves priority from the Jewish collective point of view, because it is an active player in history and because it responds to the national interest of the Jewish people at large.[5] However, Israel's primacy vis-à-vis the emancipated Diaspora does not mean that the two cannot coexist. Indeed, in Rotenstreich's opinion, the metaphor of primacy (the Hebrew term that he used, *bekhora*, denotes the privilege of the first-born) alludes nicely to the dynamic direction in which Israel-Diaspora relations are developing.

In Rotenstreich's thinking, the preferential status of the State of Israel is self-evident; Israel earned it as a manifestation of the collective Jewish will. Here, too, one may discern the seminal nature of his voluntaristic outlook. The focal question, in his opinion, is whether the Jewish people will be politically free and whether it will bear the burden of state sovereignty. These factors are crucial for Jewry's continued existence, since in their absence it will be "absorbed into the universal culture of the modern world." Therefore, the nation's will to continue existing and to shape its existence creatively lies in the center of his Zionist outlook: ". . . We are struggling . . . [with the question of] whether the Jewish people, as a historical unit, will continue to act from its existential sources or will exist on the fringes the world, and in the best case symbolic patterns of Jewish existence will remain. . . . Do we want symbolic vestiges of existence [traditional, religious, and other] or do we want an existence composed of a tapestry of [national] activity, including [the nation's] creative tapestry?"[6]

Prompted by his commitment to the continued collective existence of the Jewish people and the vitality of its cultural creativity, Rotenstreich adopted what we have called the "inside intellectual" pattern—the critical posture of a fearless intellectual who is undaunted by practical considerations and remains true to the vital interests of the Jewish people as he sees them. Below we assess Rotenstreich's pungent criticism of the formational Israeli society during the early statehood years and of its leaders, members of his party, Mapai. Here we note that he did not hesitate to dash American Jews' hopes of establishing a "new Babylon" in their own country. Sorrowfully, without gloating, but without pulling punches, he stated that America had not evolved into a creative Jewish center and that all the immense intellectual forces of American Jewry were being pledged to sustaining, and not to enhancing, the Jewish framework.[7] The tenor of the remarks indicates that they were written from the perspective of an "insider" who approached the issue with profound empathy but without self-delusion.

Thus, Rotenstreich also exhibits an inferential voluntarism based on the Jews' collective will to exist and on mobilizing the will of individual Jews (halutsim) to sustain their national existence. Also evident is his Socialist outlook, which focuses on the rational will of a society composed of free individuals who share full responsibility for their society. An essential synthesis of Zionism and Socialism, in the typical manner of the Zionist Labor Movement, is evident in Rotenstreich, as stated. Now we can understand the way Rotenstreich crafted this synthesis. Thus, in his political outlook, the voluntary shaping of reality is the main link between Zionism and Socialism—the link that makes the Zionist-Socialist synthesis possible. Both Zionism and Socialism are important manifestations, as stated, of the same voluntaristic foundation in Rotenstreich's thought—the striving for collective self-determination by way of shaping society and national existence.

In Rotenstreich's opinion, a worthy society is one "in which duties are honored voluntarily," that is, not due to enforcement, and one that upholds the entitlements of its disadvantaged members. The fundamental of service for the collective shows plainly that Jewish collective existence in Israel is aimed against "the automatic nature of the flow of life" and is rooted in worldviews and consciousness. Admittedly, Zionism is not an all-embracing ethical or philosophical worldview, but "an attempt by the Jewish people to sustain its collective reality within the history of the world as it is." By inference, however, ". . . it also turns its attention to [the fate of] Jewish individuals." Therefore, according to Rotenstreich, Zionism itself "leads . . . to the principle of social solidarity." Unless Israeli society is guided by this principle, it will be a society "torn not only from its Socialist roots but also from its [Zionist] roots," since, in his opinion, "There is a connection between way of life and social orientation and the principal motives of Zionism." The solidarity that Zionism affirms is based on the application of the collective authority on individuals' behalf but contradicts any tendency by individuals to live at the collective's expense.[8] But as we saw, the Zionist and the Socialist roots of the Israeli society are in Rotenstreich's thought two manifestations of the demand that the Jews will control their social and national fate.

A good way to make further progress in assessing the nature of voluntarism in Rotenstreich's thinking is to study his critique of Marx's sweeping historicization of the concept of "human nature." As Rotenstreich expressed it, Marx went so far afield in his extreme historicistic tendency that he identified everything in human history with passing historical outcomes. Human reality, however, does not boil down to things that people create and social relations that they form in accordance with the material production method. Neither does it boil down to the ideas that man creates in view of these social relations. In Rotenstreich's opinion, Marx reached this reductionistic conclusion by adopting a premise that was even more inclusively reductionistic: the perception of everything in human reality, "everything that exists on a man's horizon," as man-made. Thus, a person perceives the entire reality in which he/she lives as a human reality that he/she "made."[9]

Rotenstreich strove to undermine the deterministic assumptions of Marx in order to leave room for a voluntaristic and emancipatory philosophy that focused on the concept of rational will. He wanted to leave room for the Kantian concept of rational will, which lay at the theoretical center of his Zionist Socialism. His basic claim is that Marx overstated his case by applying the historical category so totally as to assume that the dialectic progression of history would resolve even contrasts that, in Rotenstreich's opinion, are essentially ahistorical, such as "the contrast of man as an autonomous being and the world that surrounds him, to which he belongs but from which, nevertheless, he is different." This contrast, in Rotenstreich's thinking, cannot be considered a historical contrast such as property versus labor. Rotenstreich also believed that even contrasts of lesser magnitude than that between individual autonomy and individual inclusion in the world—such as the clash between individual and collective or that between the individual's ability and his/her will—are indicators of human nature and not of transient phases in human history. Here he takes issue with Marx's claim that "all history is nothing but a continuous transformation of human nature."[10] All contradictions that the historical dialectic cannot resolve are indicators of prehistoric human nature and, for this reason, will also be indicators of posthistoric human nature, that is, a human nature that would persist after all the contradictions are "resolved."

Rotenstreich wished to posit the action of rational will in these gaps between the poles of the natural, history-transcending contradictions. He sought to prove that conscious rational action is essential for personal and collective emancipation in all phases of history and will always remain so. Consequently, the fundamental of voluntarism in Rotenstreich's thinking—a very meaningful element in his Zionist and Socialist thought—was deeply rooted in his philosophical thought as well.

We cannot follow all avenues of discussion about the critique of Marx's historicism here, of course. Therefore, we conclude by defining the pioneering voluntarism of the left-wing Zionists as the concrete manifestation of this critique, even though no few carriers of *halutsiyut*, Zionist pioneerism, considered themselves Marxists. Rotenstreich's thinking may shed clearer light on the true nature of voluntarism in left-wing Zionism.

Rotenstreich's *Criticism of Early Israeli Society*

Nathan Rotenstreich was one of the most prominent critics in Mapai's internal debate about political institutionalization at the outset of Israeli independence. His critique centered on the vitiation of halutsiyut, that is, the weakening of society's voluntaristic nature. Rotenstreich's first fierce criticism of the political institutionalization that occurred in the early independence years appeared in an article titled "Israeli Society in Crisis" (October 1950). The article expressed the harsh feelings that prompted Rotenstreich, and many other participants in the internal ideological debate in Mapai, to criticize Mapai caustically for the form it had acquired and the way it managed the state's affairs. Here Rotenstreich again demonstrated his independent spirit amid other critics, no less acrid, among the Mapai ideologues of the time.

Rotenstreich's commitment to the "primacy of will," guided by reason, seems to have diminished the political effectiveness of his analyses. Rotenstreich urged the party to extricate itself from the institutionalization crisis by applying realistic critical thinking, free of cynical skepticism and self-satisfaction. Although his article reverberated widely, it led to no conclusion save a series of moral exhortations. The heads of state should laud kibbutz society. The kibbutz movement should withdraw from "the frenzy of financial corruption that has gripped Israeli society" in its outward behavior and not only in the management of its internal affairs. Mapai should stanch "the frenzy of selfishness in class or institutional garb" and should demand that its members lead a modest lifestyle. The leaders of government should become paragons of "return to a simple life, i.e., the dominion of the idea." It is hard to resist the conclusion that Rotenstreich's critical power in this article surpassed his ability to propose a way to solve the crisis. Nevertheless, one cannot but respect the voluntaristic moral ethos that guided him.[11]

The atmosphere of crisis and alarm also stands out in the article "About the Horizon of Time in Our Lives," which Rotenstreich published in June 1951, several weeks before the Second Knesset elections and apparently due to the anxiety that beset Mapai officials before this event. Here, among all aspects of the social crisis that he identified at the time, Rotenstreich focused on "bourgeoisization." In contrast to the allegations, accusations, and preachings that filled his earlier article, "Israeli Society in Crisis," Rotenstreich now took a more sober approach. Appreciating the intensity of the objective processes that had engendered the contemporaneous crises and realizing that preaching would not be useful, he admitted that the crises of "the day after" were unavoidable and more powerful than the countering force that Ben-Gurion and his colleagues in the government could apply. (In October 1950, Pinchas Lavon, leader of the Gordonia group in Mapai, the branch with which Rotenstreich was affiliated, had joined the government.) It is interesting to see how a noted anti-determinist such as Rotenstreich,[12] who attributed much importance to social engineering prompted by idea-driven will and spearheaded by a voluntary movement, was forced to acknowledge the predetermination of social processes that resulted from voluntary formative decisions of the leadership under Ben-Gurion.

Just the same, Rotenstreich warned that the "bourgeoisization" of the Jewish workers, along with the rest of society, would endanger the very existence of Israeli society, narrow its time horizon, lower its morale, and ultimately impair its security. To revive Israeli society, he wrote—in an article published about a month before the elections—Mapai and its leadership should banish considerations of popularity from their thinking and revert to the wellsprings of the Labor Movement, viz, to prefer the value of labor over the value of standard of living, to serve society instead of exploiting it, and to prefer voluntary bottom-up awakening over top-down guidance by means of rules and regulations.[13]

About a year later, in late 1951, Rotenstreich published another article in *Molad*, "The First Pincer," in which he expressed different attitudes toward the role of the state in view of the erosion of the voluntaristic norms, the crisis of halutsiyut. In his October 1950 article, "Israeli Society in Crisis," Rotenstreich attributed most of the blame for the crisis to the state and its leaders. Now, after the general elections, he placed his trust in these very players and urged them to be the "first pincer" in extricating the pioneering movement from its emergency.

Rotenstreich likened the country's populace to "a mass of individuals at each other's throats. The Yishuv is behaving . . . like a society that no longer believes in its future and, accordingly, is indulging in a feeding frenzy." The immigrants, in Rotenstreich's judgment, have given the nonimmigrants a human and social alibi. The gist of this alibi, he wrote, is the assumption that since the country's human quality is about to decline in any case, it is best to live for the moment and maximize one's pleasure in so doing. However, he continued, it is the nonimmigrants, not the immigrants, who are the source of the immigrant-absorption problems. Successful immigrant absorption integrates newcomers into living institutions that teach them behavior patterns that the immigrants would perceive as "parts of the natural landscape that should be taken for granted." Instead of this, Israel's nonimmigrants are exchanging all their institutions, their social orders, their values, and their own social ethic for loose change. They have become a "collection of individuals [that] lacks the strength to absorb [immigrants]." A faceless community that confronts another faceless community lacks the prime condition for absorption, Rotenstreich wrote piercingly. Momentarily abandoning his typical voluntarism, he admitted, "There is no hope for a moral turnaround without the assurance of a known minimum supply. . . . [Absent this, people] will regard themselves as fighting for life itself and will consider all means fit. . . ." He hurriedly added, however, that the main need was "to put together core groups of people who will maintain the cohesion of the veteran Yishuv and, by so doing, sustain its institutions, without which the masses of immigrants will not be absorbed." In other words, a pioneering elite should be established and the government should be responsible for establishing it. Thus, overlooking the disapproval of the state that typified his article, "Israeli Society in Crisis," and that would typify his writings in subsequent articles (especially those in the 1960s), Rotenstreich assigned the government a normative role.[14]

In this article and others of similar intent that he published during those years, Rotenstreich expressed the main fundamental of the *mamlakhtiyut* outlook, one that recurs in all its manifestations, radical and moderate alike—the civil-national or republican-patriotic insistence that the state be an important object of its citizens' emotional identification and be recognized as a dominant player in a diverse civil society and as the setting for democratic decisionmaking in said society. Furthermore, in "The First Pincer," as we have seen, Rotenstreich even designated the state as a source of norms.

In three articles published in the spring and summer of 1952 and in early 1953, Rotenstreich attempted to devise a general way out of the impasse that he had identified between late 1950 and late 1951 and early 1952. This attempt, however, amounted to adherence to the hope that may have diverted his political thinking from practical conclusions. Thus, again he called for a renewal of the relationship between the members of the Socialist halutsic settlements and the political system. Again Rotenstreich resorted to a rather idyllic portrayal of the Yishuv past. Back then, he said, an effort had been made to blend, if not to integrate fully, the halutsic settler elite and the political elite and to recruit leadership from the ranks of those who considered their personal fate and the collective's one and the same. Thus, Rotenstreich's analysis remained within the domain of hope for the restoration of the political role of Yishuv-era pioneerism; it contained no proposals about society-building in the early independence period.[15]

One may question the political efficacy of these remarks, but Rotenstreich's independent-mindedness is strongly evident in his general criticism of Israel's nascent society and his party, Mapai, the ruling party in Israel's early years. His criticism reveals his national attachment, his social commitment, and his political affiliations. His fierce criticism was plainly the work of an "insider."

The complexity of Rotenstreich's public writing is amply evidenced in his discussions of the concept of *mamlakhtiyut*[16] in Israel's early years. He did not invest his energy in simplistic distinctions and either-or conceptual dichotomies that ostensibly set matters straight but actually render the discussion superficial. This explains the typical tension in his public writing between an inferential demand to return Israeli society to the voluntaristic values that he cherished and a statist outlook that assigns the state and its leadership a central, that is, a normative role in the revival of pioneering voluntarism and the reinvigoration of its values. The tension in his writing mirrors the dialectic tension that existed in the historical reality of the time. In this sense, Rotenstreich's public writing, at its best, ushers us into the secret recesses of the basic contradictions that typified the "Israeli condition" during the country's founding years.

Zionism in the Era of *Mamlakhtiyut*

The demographic disaster of the Holocaust and the achievement of Jewish statehood after the end of World War II plunged Rotenstreich's movement, the Zionist Labor Movement, into disequilibrium. As a pioneering movement, it had lost its main source of vitality, the left-wing Zionist youth in Poland, after having been cut off from Russian-Jewish youth since the 1920s. However, its two main political parties, Mapai and Mapam,[17] became the largest political force in Israel[18] and Mapai spearheaded the construction and shaping of Israeli society. Furthermore, from that time and for more than a generation, the Zionist Labor Movement, with Mapai at its head, was able to influence relations between Israel and a *Klal Yisrael* in which Israel was included, that is, between Israel and the Jewish people in the Diasporas.

Thus, the pioneering movement of Labor Zionism gradually exited the stage of Jewish history, whereas the large party of Labor Zionism, Mapai, became a leading force and a ruling party in a newly established sovereign state. By enacting the Law of Return (1950), Mapai created a constitutional mold that transformed the historical status of Diaspora Jewry. The Law of Return allowed Jews anywhere to acquire citizenship in the homeland in addition to their civil status in their countries of birth. This not only eradicated the phenomenon of Jewish refugeehood but also gave Jews the special privilege of choosing between two homelands. The government of Israel put this principle into practice in its immigration policies. Inspired by Zionist ideological reasoning and political interests, it brought Jewish communities and refugees to Israel, thereby practically liquidating the focal points of Jewish political and economic distress in Europe, Asia, and Africa. The mass immigration that ensued at the very outset of political independence exposed the fact that the State of Israel was the only Jewish political force that could propose large-scale solutions to the problems of Klal Yisrael.

The new phenomenon—Jewish sovereignty in the State of Israel—affected the status and condition of Klal Yisrael. However, the patterns of consciousness after sovereignty had been attained were materially different from those that typified Zionism and the Jewish people in the Diasporas during the quest for sovereignty. The Zionist conception in its Labor Movement rendition was alien to most of the immigrants, Jewish refugees and Holocaust survivors from Europe and traditional Jews from Islamic countries. Neither did this conception make deep inroads in the consciousness of Western Jews, even the young; for this reason, immigration to Eretz Israel from the West has always been meager. Additionally, there was a growing realization at the time that the threat to Jews' collective existence as members of the Jewish people would escalate commensurate with the decline in the existential threat to Jews as individuals.

Now, for the first time in its history, the Zionist Movement faced free Western Jewry alone, without East European Jewry, that highly diverse collective that had had a profound national consciousness, the Jewish collective for which the satisfaction of Jewish national interests had become a condition for the resolution of members' personal problems. In contrast, the Western Jewish tradition, including the Zionism of Western Jews, was typified by an attempt, by no means easy, to integrate two interests that did not always coincide even though they may not have been irreconcilable: the collective Jewish interest and the main concern of Western Jews, the individual Jew's interest in assuring his/her civil rights.

The disappearance of East European Jewry from the Jewish collective scene, due to the Holocaust and the Communism-imposed disengagement from the Jews of Russia, was a new historical phenomenon that the Zionist Labor Movement struggled to digest. The movement's leaders and intellectuals, raised in the national and political culture of Eastern Europe, continued to hope that they could create a spearhead halutsic movement among Western Jews. They searched for a "promotive compromise," applying a synthetic political approach that would allow them to adjust to reality without totally abandoning their Utopian vision. Nathan Rotenstreich was a pronounced adherent of this political tradition. His public writing, although realistic, did not lose visual contact with the Utopian Zionist and social horizon. This is the backdrop of his debate with a fellow "Utopian realist" in his movement, the founder-leader of the State of Israel, David Ben-Gurion, during Israel's first decade. The two of them stood out among the Mapai personalities who attempted to ordain a "promotive compromise" between the constraints of reality and the Zionist vision.

In a nutshell, one may say that Ben-Gurion had drawn a conclusion: Zionism in its old format is irrelevant for the Jewish people—both the majority, those in the West, and the minority, refugees from Europe and the Islamic countries who were moving to Israel. Therefore, after several ideological twists and turns, Ben-Gurion disengaged from the Zionist Movement and limited his affiliation to the Jewish people. In 1953, he demonstratively resigned from the World Zionist Organization and attempted to set forth a new Zionist ideology. Ben-Gurion now tried to base the aspiration to and consolidation of Jewish *mamlakhtiyut* in Israel; that is, the focus of the Zionist ideology in his eyes, on a messianic outlook rooted in the Bible. He abandoned the Second Aliya Zionism of his early years, which merged the national-collective interest and the personal interest into an inseparable whole. In its stead, he attempted to tailor the Zionist political ideal to the consciousness of his contemporaneous addressees, the newly landed immigrants in Israel and the Jews of the West, foremost those in the United States. The group affiliation of all these Jews was based on an essentially religious consciousness—traditional or Reform, but religious. Thus, Ben-Gurion resorted to the Biblical messianism that presumably united, for example, American Jews—Reform, Conservative, or Modern Orthodox—and Yemenite Jews. Below we dwell briefly on Ben-Gurion's ideological proposal. We note here, however, that Nathan Rotenstreich, a young scholar and philosopher at the time, was the only intellectual in the Labor Movement who confronted Ben-Gurion's old-new theory. He did so directly and indirectly, offering an alternative to Ben-Gurion's proposal and serving as Ben-Gurion's interlocutor in a debate on the issue of Zionism and Jewish existence.

In Rotenstreich's opinion, Klal Yisrael was liable to disintegrate in the absence of Jewish coalescence around a collective national will, that is, without autoemancipation. Thus, he attempted to apply Leon Pinsker's formula in a different Jewish reality. Pinsker had spoken of the autoemancipation of Jews who suffered from political repression and of those who had recently been given equal civil rights. Rotenstreich, in contrast, demanded the autoemancipation of post-emancipation Jews in the liberal Western democracies, whose personal civil emancipation was firmly grounded. Rotenstreich's intention in making this proposal was to add a stage in the dialectic process of Jewish national emancipation: after the transition from the universalistic principle of emancipation to the Zionist national principle of autoemancipation, he proposed that the free Western Jews move on to a phase of auto-post-emancipation surrounding the Jewish collective effort to develop the State of Israel.

At the end of World War II, in 1944–1945, when the magnitude of the Holocaust became clear, Rotenstreich realized that Zionism would now have to interact with a Diaspora that was different from East European Jewry in political status and spiritual essence. He noticed that American Jewry, although having fervently supported the establishment of a Jewish state in Palestine since the Biltmore conference in 1942, distinguished between Jewish sovereignty in Palestine and the ingathering of all Jews there. Rotenstreich, unlike Pinsker, did not consider the establishment of a Jewish state the crowning achievement in Jewish Autoemancipationism.[19]

In contrast to nearly all American Jews—Zionists and non-Zionists alike—who contented themselves with the achievement of Jewish statehood, Rotenstreich championed a pan-Jewish autoemancipationist outlook. The crux of this view is a threefold autoemancipation of Klal Yisrael: emancipation from political enslavement by means of the restoration of national sovereignty; emancipation from the menace of fragmentation and dispersion by ingathering large segments of Jewry in the historical homeland; and emancipation from the menace of cultural assimilation. In the early 1950s, Rotenstreich believed that Jews outside of Israel would remain in *Galut* (a state of exile) until Klal Yisrael achieved emancipation from the hazards of fragmentation, dispersion, and assimilation by means of a national awakening in the emancipated Diasporas.

Here the term "Galut" denotes an opposite pole to one of the basic fundamentals in Rotenstreich's thinking, that is, the opposite of his characteristic national and social voluntarism. Diaspora Jews live in Galut, exile, insofar as their lives are typified by such an extreme passivity that they fail to unite around a shared collective will for action and insofar as they go about their personal affairs in a state of inertia—separatist, dispersed, and even assimilated, unguided by a national and social vision. Jews in enlightened countries may call their Galut a "Diaspora," yet in Rotenstreich's opinion they remain in exile and shall so remain until a large proportion of world Jewry is ingathered in Israel and until the assimilation trend that typifies the realities of Diaspora life undergoes a fundamental change.

However, Rotenstreich did not believe that the Diaspora was about to liquidate itself. Furthermore, the shaping ethos of Klal Yisrael, in his view, should contain an acknowledgment of anomaly, an awareness that Jewish national existence is not normal and that only part of the nation will dwell in its sovereign state. The other part will live under one of two conditions—exile, a state of indifference to the menace to its collective existence, or an emancipated Diaspora, that is, autoemancipation by dint of collective will. Either way, in exile or in an emancipated Diaspora, Klal Yisrael will not be like all other peoples. However, although it will be characterized by division between sovereign center and dispersion, it will insist—so Rotenstreich hoped—on being one people.

Therefore, even after various Diasporas are liquidated by mass immigration, other Diasporas will continue to exist. The question, according to Rotenstreich, is whether these will be emancipated Diasporas that crystallize around a Jewish collective will even though they live outside of Israel. In a departure from the thinking of many Zionists, Rotenstreich acknowledged the success of the emancipation of Western and, in particular, American Jewry. However, he wished to direct the concern of Zionist education toward the fear that flowed from this success, the risk that Jewry would vanish due to cultural assimilation. Accordingly, he believed it possible to encourage a dialogue between the two segments of the nation—that in its homeland and that elsewhere—only after it is agreed that Jewish education in the West should be predicated on explicit negation of the premise that the emancipation has solved the Jewish problem in the Diaspora. Once this premise is negated, one could acquiesce in the historical phenomenon of the existence of parallel Jewish lives in the United States and in Israel while fighting the exilic—that is, the collectively passive—manifestations of Jewish life in the U.S.; to fight assimilation and disengagement from Klal Yisrael.[20]

Rotenstreich wanted Jewish education in the Diaspora to instill the principle of "negation of Galut" (negation of passivity and assimilation) in order to sustain an emancipated, collectively active, Jewish Diaspora. At first glance, Rotenstreich's counsel seems grossly contradictory. In fact, however, there is no contradiction here because, according to Rotenstreich, the very existence of a liberated, post-emancipationist Diaspora entails alertness to the risk of Galut, exile, that threatens the Diaspora. Therefore, he prescribed adherence to the "negation of Galut" outlook and the cultivation of an active national consciousness among Diaspora Jews. In his eyes, the "negation of Galut," the negation of collective passivity and assimilation, is above all a vital interest of the emancipated Diaspora itself.

In other words, Rotenstreich suggested a new historical and religious meaning for the term Galut. The traditional meanings were: Galut as exile from Eretz Israel and as a state of political persecutions and social discrimination; Galut as a spiritual metaphysical state of mind of a people who are longing to return to their homeland. Rotenstreich added to these two traditional meanings a new approach—Galut as a state of collective and individual Jewish passivitiy. He accepted the second definition of Galut (as Ben Halpern expressed it, "without Galut there is no redemption"). But he denied the total negation of Galut, as it was expressed by the radical Zionists, and in this case, by David Ben-Gurion. From this point of view, in our opinion, Rorenstreich added an original definition of the term Galut at the time of 'post-emancipation.'

Rotenstreich realized that this educational pattern—fostering the "negation of Galut," in the sense of negation of collective passivity and assimilation—would be suited to only a minority of Diaspora Jews and considered it a conduit to an interim phase in the history of the Zionist Movement, a phase that would last until the ingathering-of-exiles vision could be fulfilled. His acknowledgment that appropriate Zionist education could be imparted to a minority of Western Jews only was fully shared by Ben-Gurion and the kibbutz movements in the activist Left.

From this standpoint, one may understand Rotenstreich's criticism in 1950 of those who wished to implement Ahad Ha'am's spiritual-center theory in the new reality. His point of departure was the dichotomization of two concepts: *shlihut* (mission) and *halutsiyut* (pioneerism). The spiritual-center idea, Rotenstreich said, entails a mission to the Diaspora Jewish masses by a minority living under full national conditions. Pioneerism, in contrast, is an act undertaken by a handful of pioneers on the premise that the public at large will eventually be able to participate actively in it. Pioneerism, it follows, presumes the equivalence of all segments of the nation, even if their actions are not equal, and in this respect it contributes to national unity. The sense of mission attributed to Ahad Ha'am does not presume such an equivalence, since it assumes that most of the nation, or the Diasporas, will remain dependent on the minority that inhabits the center, which is located in the Land of Israel. The result, Rotenstreich wrote, is that "The Diaspora Jews remain perpetual consumers. They are a periphery not only in the physical sense but also in the human sense."

Some thirty years later, the ideologues of the Jewish center in the Diaspora would raise this claim against Ahad Ha'am and the centrality-of-Israel doctrine. For Rotenstreich, however, the argument was meant to prod emancipated Jews to take autoemancipationist action that would connect them with Israel as equal partners. Dependency on a spiritual center in Israel could not spare them from the menace of total cultural assimilation, Rotenstreich believed. Only an act of autoemancipation surrounding the Israel connection could accomplish that, and ultimately it would also lead them to ingather in Israel.[21] One might say that Rotenstreich formulated an updated and equilibrated Zionism. On the one hand, he proposes that the activist and emancipating element in Zionism not be implemented solely by action in Israel, as Ben-Gurion believed, since the activization of the Diaspora is also possible. On the other hand, developing the State of Israel is one of the most important elements in the activization of the Diaspora that Rotenstreich proposes.

Rotenstreich's unifying conception of pioneerism determined his stance in the debate over the status of the World Zionist Organization (WZO) in Israel.[22] He inveighed against the tendency of some American Zionists, foremost Abba Hillel Silver and Emanuel Neumann, to give the WZO an autonomous status, because he rejected the basis of this tendency, a Diasporist ideology that accepts without protest the fragmentation and dispersion of the Jewish people. However, since Israel sovereignty applies only to a minority of the Jewish people, Rotenstreich also dismissed Ben-Gurion's proposal that the State of Israel supplant the WZO.

In respect to Israel–Diaspora relations, Rotenstreich sought to distinguish between two types of state power: the power to decide and the power to act. The former is principled and absolute, the latter practical and relative. In other words, wherever the State of Israel and its citizens are concerned, the supreme right to decide belongs to the state and cannot be divided or shared with Diaspora Jewry. World Jewry's power to act or to take an initiative in the State's affairs is another matter entirely. Here, Israel–Diaspora cooperation is both possible and desired—provided, of course, that the right to decide remain with the state in this regard as well. To promote the desired cooperation, Rotenstreich proposed the establishment of a Jewish "upper chamber" composed of Diaspora and Israel delegates. The state, he believed, should propose the formation of such a representative body even in the knowledge that Diaspora Jewry will reject it lest it be accused of "dual loyalty."

Rotenstreich proposed the unification under one umbrella of the characteristically Jewish multitude of ways of life. Similarly, he proposed a restructuring of the WZO. The WZO, he said, should be an alliance between Israel and Diaspora Jewry, in which the former is represented by means of its legislative institution and not by voluntary political parties. "This would express the singular difference between the Zionists of Israel, who are Zionists within a political bloc, and other Zionists," he wrote. What is more, the enlistment of the institutions of state and of Zionism would stress Israel's Zionist nature. Rotenstreich knew that such an alliance would not be easy to establish and that in many senses it would be uncomfortable for Diaspora Jewry and Israel alike. "It cannot possibly be a comfortable alliance," he admitted, "because the reality that it reflects is not simple but multifarious and strewn with difficulties." What was needed, he said, was not a quest for comfort but the acknowledgment of the existing social and political diversity, since "the constitution should reflect Jewish sociology and not disregard it."

Rotenstreich's party, Mapai, took a different stance on the desired Israel–WZO relationship at the time. The party leader, Ben-Gurion, even held an "Israel-centric" republican outlook that would have placed all sovereign power in the hands of the elected Israeli institutions. Rotenstreich's membership in Mapai, however, did not deter him from proposing that the pan-Jewish representative organ be granted a special status in Israel. His proposed upper chamber would acquire some of the state's sovereign powers, albeit on a limited scale and applied solely to Israel–Diaspora relations. Ben-Gurion opposed this for political and principled reasons.

Thus, Rotenstreich took issue with Ben-Gurion's outlook in regard to the status of the WZO. Ben-Gurion agreed that it should be given a limited official status in Israel; Rotenstreich attempted to find a formula for a setting that would create an organic union between Israel and a combination of the WZO and other Jewish organizations. Hence his proposal to link the Knesset, representing the Jewish collective will in Israel, with the Zionist Movement in the Diaspora, reflecting the will of individual Jews within the unifying ambit of the WZO. The proposal bore some resemblance to an overture by Ben-Gurion, immediately after statehood was achieved, that would have created a linkage between the Zionist Executive and the institutions of state. Rotenstreich's linkage, however, was proposed in acknowledgment of diversity; the purpose of Ben-Gurion's proposal was to create unity. Rotenstreich's intent, then, was not to impose the state's will on the Zionist Movement but to create conditions for partnership of both entities under one roof.

Just the same, in Rotenstreich's view, the WZO would be entitled to a unifying status in Jewish and Israeli life only if it acknowledged "that the Jewish question has not been solved [and] that the Jewish question pertains to all Jews indiscriminately." Zionists are distinct from non-Zionist supporters of Israel in that they apply the "Jewish question" not only to Jews in distress but also to those in comfort and link the answer to the State of Israel. Only a WZO that espouses this ideology is entitled to a special status; otherwise, it "destroys by its own actions the value of its demand and the sustaining strength of the demand" to represent the Jewish people both in Israel and in the Diaspora. Such a WZO is no different from any other organization of Jews who wish to help Israel. Accordingly, it is precisely now, in the postemancipation era, that the WZO should become the representative of Klal Yisrael. Now of all times, and in the Western countries of all places, attention should be focused on the threats to Klal Yisrael that emancipation cannot solve and that only voluntaristic autoemancipationist Zionism can confront.

True to this outlook, Rotenstreich criticized Simon Rawidowicz's theory of absolute equality and equilibrium between the center in Israel and the Diaspora as a historical phenomenon that is a prerequisite for Jewish existence. From this perspective, the Jewish people may continue to exist in perpetuity only if it has multiple centers, not one center. In the new reality of the statehood era, Jewish existence resembles not a circle with Israel in its center but rather an ellipse with Israel at one point and the Diaspora at the other. For Rawidowicz, Israel and the Diaspora are "two that are one."[23]

This is not to deny that Rotenstreich and Rawidowicz agreed on several basic premises: the Jews' dispersion endangered their national existence and collective cohesion. The Jewish problem is one everywhere, with no substantive differentiation among forms of existence. All segments of Jewry are of equal value; this awareness on the part of both thinkers is connected with their opposition to Ahad Ha'am's spiritual-center doctrine. Rotenstreich, however, distinguished between relative equality and absolute equality and gave the State of Israel a special status as an instrument with which the Jewish problem might be solved. He agreed with Rawidowicz that "no segment among the segments of Jewry has intrinsic value" in dissociation from its value to the Jewish people at large. However, he argued that where the Jewish state was at issue, the segment gathered in Israel had an advantage of national value over all other segments, "because the entire Jewish fate depends on the achievement and success of the operation with which this segment is charged." This led him to express an important postulate: "Jewish unity is not only reconcilable with preference of the State of Israel and what it stands for over any other interest in Jewish life, but it also requires this preference." For this reason, Rotenstreich categorically dismissed Rawidowicz's claim that the recognition of equivalence offered a solution to the bedeviling problems of Jewish existence. The segments of Jewry, he ruled, are equivalent in some senses but not in terms of the overall national interest. Therefore, "As long as the decisive factor in our calculus is the overall national significance of Jewish life in its diverse forms, we are unlikely to come to anything but consideration of the Diasporas, but we will not arrive at giving them equal status in an overall national sense." By saying this, he dealt a blow to the most precious postulate in the diasporist ideology.

Rotenstreich's stance stemmed from the deepest root of his public thinking in general, that is, his characteristic rational voluntarism. Indeed, it was in this vein that he explained, almost twelve years later in controversial remarks during the first Israeli–American dialogue (1962), why he invested the State of Israel with an advantage of national value. Israel, he explained, is a fact created by a spiritual aspiration. Every other form of Jewish life, in contrast, however important and influential, is but a fact, albeit a "fortunate fact." Thence Rotenstreich argued that the State of Israel is the only form of Jewish life in which a Jewish collectivity is the shaping force—the only form that is shaped in all senses by the Jewish collective will. American Jewry, in contrast, is a collection of Jewish individuals who associate in order to maintain a limited collective life within their own confines. He then outraged his American interlocutors by transcending this distinction to argue that Diaspora Jewry's goal is Jewish survival whereas Israeli society's is the maintenance of creative life.[24]

Rotenstreich gradually recanted this view over the next decade or so, due to the rough if not angry criticism that his remarks evoked among American-Jewish intellectuals, on the one hand, and the development of Israel–Diaspora relations after the Six-Day War and the Yom Kippur War, on the other hand. Jewish solidarity was indeed salient and the premise of Jewish unity was validated in both wars, but the growing influence of the Diaspora was underscored as well. Under the new circumstances, Rotenstreich proposed that the traditional Zionist formula of Israel's centrality in the Jewish world be relinquished; it had "worn itself out and become overly banal," he said. In its stead, he proposed an alternative definition of Israel's status: "Firstness of Israel, preference of Israel, primacy of Israel vis-a-vis the Diaspora in a material sense."[25]

This formula, Rotenstreich explained, means that the State of Israel is neither a center that imposes its authority on the periphery nor a weak and threatened entity that relies on the Diaspora. The existence of the State of Israel is an interest of all of Jewry, including, of course, the Diasporas. By struggling for the state's existence, Klal Yisrael struggles for its own survival and collective existence. Thus, one who helps to fight Israel's existential wars is not offering charity to beleaguered brethren but rather tackling a national problem or conflict that involves the entire Jewish people. The conflict is the result of the Jews' conscious collective decision to restore their national sovereignty and maintain it by means of an effort and a concern that Israel and the Diaspora share. Therefore, it is in the interest of all segments of Jewry, of Klal Yisrael, to wage this struggle. Even now, in the 1970s, Rotenstreich wished to maintain a

Diaspora of strong national consciousness, a partner of the State of Israel, on the one hand, and to preserve the living Israel–Diaspora relationship by means of pioneering immigration of Jews, numerically small but driven by the potency of the Zionist goal, on the other hand.

Rotenstreich's view of the primacy of Israel as the supreme manifestation of the Jewish collective will does not imply that Rotenstreich considered Diaspora Jewry a passive player only and that, for this reason, he discredited Jewish existence in the Diaspora. Indeed, "There is no doubt," he stated in the mid-1950s, "that the will of Jews in the Western Diaspora to exist as Jews is a forceful and dynamic one that motivates them to act and enables them to withstand the ordeals of their environment and its development." The collective will, however, is the only national basis that Diaspora Jewry still possesses. It has long ago lost other bases of national existence in dispersion, objective ones such as a unique language, regional concentration, a comprehensive set of institutions, and even a standard religious pattern. Ultimately, too, Rotenstreich stated, the objective reality will undoubtedly win its confrontation with the subjective Jewish will.

". . . The Jewish concentration in Israel," he continued by way of contrast, "requires Jews there to reposition themselves objectively within the realm of Jewish history and to live within the Jewish historical horizon." Since Diaspora Jewry has no such obligation, to put it mildly, their historical consciousness "contracts" and their connection with the State of Israel is limited to the political, economic, and emotional planes. The connection has not had the privilege of being perfected and reinforced by ideological coordination, Rotenstreich explained, because Jews in the free Diaspora are afraid to define themselves ideologically. Such a definition might create a buffer between them and their surroundings, "whereas their entire every day interest is to cling to the given surroundings." Therefore, Rotenstreich said, "Diaspora Jewry tends to complement its real wish [to integrate into its surroundings] by invoking the status of the State of Israel as representative of the plane of Jewish life, without making . . . [Jewish] history a concrete part of its way and its consciousness."

The result is that Israel has risen in status on the Jewish scene but has not done so on the basis of a shared consciousness. This, according to Rotenstreich, is an undesirable development in overall national terms, since the interests of Klal Yisrael entail ideological unity or shared consciousness. Rotenstreich did not welcome the development of an external relationship with Israel; he was one of those who aspired to Jewish national coalescence based on shared consciousness. To attain such a consciousness, he attempted to foster the recognition by Klal Yisrael of Israel's objective superiority in the national sense, due to its being a valid instrumentality for the solution of the "Jewish question" wherever Jews are a minority. Rotenstreich thought it possible on the basis of this ideological unity to create a unity of national action by means of a shared institutional setting that would invest Jews with an inclusive historical consciousness and a link between their past and their present and future.

Rotenstreich's historical outlook drew him into a public debate with Ben-Gurion over Israel's station on the continuum of Jewish history. The debate, conducted in the form of a public exchange of letters, began shortly before the Sinai Campaign and continued after it, that is, before the personal split that occurred in 1960 between Ben-Gurion and Lavon, the leader of Rotenstreich's political faction. As stated, Ben-Gurion postulated that the new conditions had invalidated the Zionist ideology as it had developed under the special circumstances of Eastern Europe at a particular time. This ideology, Ben-Gurion claimed, did not speak to the Jewish masses and could not capture the hearts of youth. In its stead, Ben-Gurion argued, young people should be given "a Jewish consciousness that draws its nourishment from the great spiritual heritage of the Jewish people, which binds all segments of Jewry everywhere in a partnership of fate, be it conscious or unconscious, and from the messianic vision, the vision of Jewish and human redemption bequeathed to us by the Prophets of Israel." It was this messianic vision, culled from the Bible, that motivated the early harbingers and fulfillers of Zionism—so Ben-Gurion believed—and only by its means could one fully understand the miracle of the founding of Israel and the ingathering of the exiles. In a nutshell, "The climate of the Bible is the climate of our lives"; it is more appropriate for the way of life of Israelis today, and does more to shape their lives, than the Talmud, the medieval literature, and the Zionist ideology. Thus, Ben-Gurion believed in the possibility of disengagement from the historical continuum. He argued vehemently that a "historical leap" into the future could in fact occur and wished to make this leap with the Biblical heritage in his luggage.

Rotenstreich, in contrast, believed that consciousness of the need for a homeland was insufficient as a basis. ". . . If we relieve the young person in the homeland of the objective yoke of the 'Zionist' perspective, i.e., of regarding his duties as part of the Jewish *klal* [the Jewish people at large], then instead of strengthening his roots in the natural and given homeland we will in fact have weakened them." The reason is that "this unburdening carries the risk of depriving the inhabitant of the homeland of the historical and psychological rationale for the very existence of the homeland." The messianic consciousness, in Rotenstreich's opinion, lacks this historical rationale. The Zionist "realistic consciousness" corrects this drawback because it developed as a product of the requirements of the Jewish reality of recent generations—and not of the reality of the ancient Israelites' lives. The messianic idea plays a role, but not a determining role, in the reconnection of the Jewish people with its historical land.

This is the case according to Rotenstreich, and maybe even more so, with the question of Jewish unity. The messianic idea, as construed by Ben-Gurion, cannot create a connection with the Jewish people: "The connection [of Israel] with the Jews [of the Diaspora] in the present is meaningless without a perspective on the meaning of the Jewish question in its various incarnations." Moreover, the Jewish question is actually a pan-Jewish one; it concerns northern African and American Jews just as it once concerned East European Jews. Rotenstreich claimed that the historical consciousness of the Jewish question and ways to deal with it is the only focus around which Jewish unity among different communities could be attained.

These remarks of Rotenstreich's alluded to the "Canaanite" leanings that had become current among young people and, perhaps, in Ben-Gurion's own thinking; that is, the tendency to disengage from the Diaspora and focus on parochial nationhood. It was his concern about a covert or not entirely conscious "Canaanite" trend of thought that prompted him to oppose Ben-Gurion's "Biblical ideology." Distinguishing between the resurrection of an era and a historical leap over historical eras, Rotenstreich argued that it was impossible to connect with the distant past while disconnecting from the recent past: "We are resurrecting the Biblical background," Rotenstreich noted, by being erstwhile Diaspora Jews, unlike "those for whom the Diaspora is a passive and unrecorded background. . . . Here a leap is impossible, and if one occurs we will have created a Karaism of consciousness, on the one hand, and disengagement from the Jewish partnership of fate in the present, on the other hand." Ben-Gurion's leap, in Rotenstreich's opinion, carried two menaces: "of Karaism, i.e., suspension of development in disregard of temporal changes, and . . . of 'Canaanism,' which, by exaggerating its adherence to change disengages from the past, with everything this implies from the national perspective."

Rotenstreich did not categorically rule out the very possibility of such a historical leap. However, "after I leaped," he explained, "I did not nullify the physical and mental reality from which I had leaped." The leap from, or negation of, the Diaspora was "a historical necessity [in its time] for practical and psychological matters, but this does not mean that the last word on the issue has been said." In Rotenstreich's opinion, the young generation in Israel might not resemble that of its parents, who had "leaped" into a new reality; it would instead, for its own reasons, avail itself of the folk culture of the Diaspora.

Thus, Rotenstreich dismissed Ben-Gurion's belief that the "Israeli normalization" was distancing young people from their people's Jewish past. He admitted that the generation being raised in Israel tended "to think that we are already normal, and is right to some extent." However, "These changes force us to rephrase our lasting core interests but not to burn our conceptual spiritual bridges. . . . The main question is whether we can see that we are still in the very midst of the process of solving the Jewish question—and, if so, we may no longer fail to regard ourselves as tied to the Zionist background in the historical and social sense of the concept."[26] This statement seems to outshine all others in expressing the gist of the Zionist and pan-Jewish outlook that Rotenstreich had formulated after the establishment of the State of Israel.

Summing up the indirect and direct debate between Ben-Gurion and Rotenstreich, one may say that the two disputants raised separate if not clashing proposals for the shaping of Klal Yisrael after the establishment of Jewish sovereignty in Israel. Ben-Gurion despaired of the Zionist Movement and turned to Klal Yisrael in the Utopian hope that it would reinvigorate pioneering Zionism. He pinned much on this hope, considering the renewal of pioneering Zionism crucial for the resting of Jewish statehood on sustainable moral foundations. Rotenstreich, in contrast, sought to transform the Zionist Movement into a center of national enrichment and inspiration for Klal Yisrael. Thus, both aspired to the renewal of pioneering Zionism, but whereas Ben-Gurion advocated the disengagement of pioneerism from the WZO, Rotenstreich believed that pioneerism should be renewed within the WZO framework and that the genuine Zionist Movement, which the Jewish people in the Diaspora and in Israel need, should be refashioned thereby.

These disagreements led to another difference between the two disputants' outlooks. Ben-Gurion believed that the consolidation of Jewish statehood would solve the Jewish problem foremost by means of immigration and, this failing, by an unbroken relationship between Israel and Diaspora Jewry. Rotenstreich did not consider the attainment of statehood an all-inclusive national solution for Diaspora Jewry. The establishment of Jewish sovereignty per se, and it alone, he believed, did not solve the Jewish problem in an inclusive and exhaustive way. Therefore, he proposed an alternative to Ben-Gurion's suggestion that the establishment of the State of Israel offered Diaspora Jewry a "statist" emancipation. Rotenstreich's proposal was a Jewish Autoemancipation that would make the Diaspora, linked to Israel, Israel's partner in the effort to sustain the integrity and unity of Klal Yisrael and sustain it as an active collective entity in the Diaspora and in Israel. The result, in Rotenstreich's opinion, would be a partnership between unequal sides in Jewish collective terms, as may be seen in his disputation with Simon Rawidowicz. After all, the unity of Klal Yisrael hinges more on the national center in Israel than on any Diaspora or even on all the Diasporas combined. Therefore, the Klal Yisrael perception itself tips the scales toward a higher valuing of the Jewish state.

Here we encounter a fine but important distinction between Ben-Gurion's outlook on the centrality of the State of Israel for the Klal Yisrael reality and Rotenstreich's view on the same issue. During and after the pre-state era, Ben-Gurion thought the Jewish national effort should focus on the enterprise in Eretz Israel, which he considered the essence of the pan-Jewish national interest. For Rotenstreich, the preeminent focal point was the Jewish people; the State of Israel deserves preference because it is crucial for the maintenance of pan-Jewish national unity. This is why he recommended the establishment of one representative institution for the common interests of Diaspora Jewry and Israel, a proposal that Ben-Gurion opposed due to his view of Israel as the only manifestation of the Jewish collective will.

The public importance of the discourse between the two diminished steadily over time. Over the years, there were at least two junctions that demonstrated the correctness of both men's arguments. The first was the outburst of solidarity and national identification on the part of Diaspora Jewry, and especially American Jewry, during the Six-Day War. On the one hand, it was a demonstration of support from Klal Yisrael for the State of Israel, following Ben-Gurion's outlook. On the other hand, it was an autoemancipationist awakening on the part of American Jewry, the sort of development for which Rotenstreich had hoped. After the war, halutsic emigration from United States to Israel climbed to unprecedented magnitudes. American Jewry still shows the effects of this autopost-emancipationist awakening.

At the time of the Yom Kippur War (1973), concern for Israel's existence became a problem of Klal Yisrael in both the

Diaspora and Israel. This concern and its predecessor, the autoemancipationist awakening before and after the Six-Day War, caused Klal Yisrael to unite even more strongly around collective feelings and made the distinctiveness of the Zionist Movement even vaguer in contrast to the many who identified with Israel. Thus, Zionism, entrapped and embroiled in contradictions that stemmed from its historical achievements, accepted Klal Yisrael "as is" instead of serving it as a source of inspiration and ferment and a focal point for the mobilization of the Diasporas around an active national will, as Rotenstreich had hoped.

※ ※ ※

Nathan Rotenstreich was undoubtedly right in this regard: in the absence of a shared guiding and unifying idea, Klal Yisrael was endangered by its powerful centripetal trends. Paradoxically, an Israel-centric mindset contributes to the degeneration of Klal Yisrael when it is nothing but a facile and noncommittal substitute for collective coalescence around a national idea and an active national will that is materially related to the State of Israel. This happens, according to Rotenstreich, when identification with Israel in the Diaspora becomes a substitute for, instead of a manifestation of, the Zionist spirit. Rotenstreich considered the Zionist idea the most intensive, complete, and inclusive Klal Yisrael outlook in the modern historical reality. After all, the Zionist idea encompasses ideological and value fundamentals that pertain to all important segments of Klal Yisrael. It includes religious, secular, national, republican, democratic, socialist, and liberal fundamentals. Of all the various worldviews that Jews hold, only Zionism can express Klal Yisrael comprehensively. Only Zionism has a historical tradition of striving for such expression and the intellectual and conceptual strength to demand the pluralistic gathering of the diverse segments of Klal Yisrael under one national umbrella. For this reason, and due to its voluntaristic mobilizing nature and its role as a natural focal point for the coalescence of the collective Jewish will and for the organization of pioneers around such a will, Rotenstreich adhered to it amid all the historical changes that he experienced during his life.

This preliminary discussion of Rotenstreich's Zionist and Socialist worldview and his political involvement in public debates about Israel–Diaspora relations and the nature of democracy in Israel provide, in our opinion, a background that will help the reader to understand the ideas presented in this book. Importantly, Rotenstreich edited and wrote these chapters in the late 1980s and in the early 1990s, shortly before his death. Therefore, they may be viewed as his spiritual and ideological testament.

The title of the book, *Zionism Past and Present,* expresses Rotenstreich's principal idea about a dialectic relationship between past and present in Zionism. Here Rotenstreich notes the great changes that occurred in the history of Zionism but also stresses Zionism's constant and immutable principles. The entire analysis rests on a premise to which Rotenstreich adhered without hesitation: that beyond the geographic dispersion, the cultural diversity, the religious fragmentation, and the difference in civil status, there is one Jewish people that embrace the State of Israel and the Diasporas.

Rotenstreich examined this point of departure neither in its present existential sense only nor in its historical dimension only but also, and mainly, at its conceptual level, the level that transcends temporal changes. He performed this inquiry in the conviction that there is a continuity in the questions that Zionism elicited, despite revolutionary changes in the status and situation of the Jewish people that left their imprint on Jewish history for better or worse. The Jewish center in the United States has come to being, as has the Jewish state, and the Holocaust took place and the Jewish center in Europe has vanished. Nevertheless, Rotenstreich believes that certain questions, such as the attitude toward *Galut,* exile, or what has been called "negation of Galut," remain valid.

For this reason, throughout his book Rotenstreich repeatedly turns to Ahad Ha'am, the famous Zionist thinker who distinguished between "subjective negation of exile," which stresses the foreignness and malaise of the individual Jew, and "objective negation of exile," which regards exilic existence as undesirable if not uncomfortable but does not pronounce it impossible. From Rotenstreich's standpoint, the discussion of

Ahad Ha'am is neither intellectual nor historical but practical and current, since it pertains to relations between the sovereign Jewish state and a Jewish Diaspora, which, in terms of its "objective" existence in the various countries, has changed unrecognizably for the better. In Rotenstreich's view, the change is revolutionary from the standpoint of the Jewish individual, who is now almost totally free to integrate into the economy, the culture, the politics, and even the collective psyche of the surrounding society. This change, however, is insignificant in terms of the problems that Zionism has revealed in the modern era, which remain essentially unchanged. From Rotenstreich's perspective, Ahad Ha'am's classic differentiation between the "problem of the Jews" and the "problem of Judaism" is still valid and extant, since the freer the Jew becomes as an individual, the greater the menace to Jewish solidarity and the Jews' existence as a historically and currently distinct nation.

The six chapters of the book discuss the status and specialness of the Jewish people from a Zionist point of view. The chapters are grouped in two clusters. In the first three chapters, Rotenstreich engages in historical and philosophical discussion of matters of theory; the last three chapters deal with practical issues that pertain to Israel–Diaspora relations. In the first part of the book, Rotenstreich creates a conceptual infrastructure; in the second part he uses the concepts to examine the particular reality of the time.

Each of the chapters is built around three basic concepts: Return, Modernity, and Renaissance. The three concepts are examined in view of their universalistic content as it is coupled to the particularistic situation of the Jewish people. The first concept, Return, is the broadest of the three and embraces the other two, even though each stands on its own legs. Zionism is an inseparable part of modern nationalism, but the concept of Return is the particularistic indicator of Zionism in contrast to other modern national movements. Zionism was called upon to assume tasks that no national movement in Europe had attempted to undertake: to return the Jews to their historical homeland, the Land of Israel; to restore the national language, Hebrew; and to return the Jews to history as a collective that functions politically within history. This dynamic of "return," with its diverse meanings, also affects current relations between Israel and Diaspora Jewry, on the one hand, and Israel and the Arab world, especially the Palestinians, on the other hand.

The concept of "Return" is coupled with that of "Modernity." Rotenstreich believes that Modernity, in its general context, denotes secularity, emancipation, and rule of law. These meanings are augmented by the special tendencies of modernity in the Zionist Movement: the intention of territorializing the Jewish people in its historical homeland; the revival of the Hebrew language, which is linked to the specific territory of the Land of Israel; and the Zionism–Socialism nexus. It is true that the relationship of nationalism and Socialism in Zionism was typical of only part of the Zionist Movement, but that part was the most influential in the nation-building and state-building process. Furthermore, Socialism held a very important status in Zionism, if not a dominant status in certain fields, and one can hardly find a similar phenomenon in any other national movement. This phenomenon is one of the manifestations of the uniqueness of Zionism within nationalism at large.

The third concept, "Renaissance," is intellectually the most problematic because it is typified by an internal contradiction. On the one hand, it denotes a return to the past, for example, to classical civilization; on the other hand, it means change relative to the current situation. In Zionism, this is manifested in tension between two views of Renaissance. One concerns the renewal of national, cultural, and religious existence—the restoration and rebirth of the national political tradition. The second view concerns a revolutionary change in Jews' way of life, the adjustment to political sovereignty and modern society. Therefore, the tension between the existence of Jews and the existence of Judaism was aggravated in the process of fulfilling Zionism and establishing Jewish statehood.

In sum, Rotenstreich's discussion of these three basic concepts demonstrates the internal tension that flows from the combination of the universalistic and the particularistic elements that have been intrinsic in Zionism since its inception in respect to the question of the development of Klal Yisrael.

In the next three chapters of the book, as stated, Rotenstreich examines existential or practical aspects of the Israel–Diaspora relationship. The first aspect, and the main one in terms of the Zionist worldview, is the matter of "negation of exile." It stresses the fact that Zionist thinking carried on in the religious tradition of negating exile as a punishment, but instead of religious passivity toward the punishment of exile, Zionism advocated the active negation of exile as a humiliating moral phenomenon, a state of economic marginality, political discrimination, and spiritual degeneracy. Whereas the religious negation of exile was reflected in adherence to the faith and expectation of deliverance from on high, Zionism demanded political, social, and economic action to bring about deliverance here and now.

Rotenstreich, however—following Ahad Ha'am and in contradiction to Theodor Herzl—believes not in liquidating the Diaspora but in preserving it by creating a national center for the development of Jewish civilization that will also serve the Diaspora. Rotenstreich, like Ahad Ha'am nearly a century earlier, believed that the Diaspora lacks the vital force to sustain itself. Rotenstreich, like Ahad Ha'am, does not believe that Diaspora Jewry, especially in the free West, will be able to survive as a collective unless it forms a relationship with the national center in the Land of Israel, that is, the State of Israel.

However, Rotenstreich does not follow Ahad Ha'am's lead in regard to the contents of the relationship between the center in Israel and the Diasporas. He realized that the Diaspora faced by Zionism in his time was composed not of Jewish victims of discrimination but of free Jews, who not only refuse to reject exile in the "objective" sense of the term, let alone the "subjective" sense, as Ahad Ha'am reasoned, but actually affirm it.

Furthermore, Rotenstreich admits that the center that Zionism established for the Jewish people does focus Jews' attention. However, it does so not as a paragon of Jewish life but as a shelter for Jews in need, such as those from the former Soviet Union or Ethiopia. By the same token, Rotenstreich stresses the fact that a Diaspora whose consciousness lacks a national center practically rules out its autonomous existence amid the historical process of integration and social assimilation.

This is why Rotenstreich attempts to examine critically the essence of the Jewish people's national center, the values of Israeli society. In this sense, too, he follows the teachings of Ahad Ha'am, since Ahad Ha'am intended his spiritual center to be a paragon in the sense of Jewish values. Rotenstreich understood that Israel, as it verges on the new millennium, cannot serve as a spiritual center for Diaspora Jews because these Jews are well integrated into their surrounding cultures and contribute creatively to them. Therefore, he concentrated on making spiritual demands of Israeli society.

Rotenstreich points to Israel's unity-versus-pluralism dichotomy, one that is intrinsic because Israel is developing as an integrated national entity on the basis of a proliferation of culturally differentiated segments. The contradiction, of course, reflects a more general tension between the aspiration to personal welfare and the well-being of the collective to which the individual belongs and that he/she needs. Rotenstreich then discerns an additional tension in Israeli society, between the dynamic "ideology" of technological progress and national "renaissance," which denotes among other things a return to religious tradition. This phenomenon surfaced in full political fury after Rotenstreich's death, with the establishment of Shas, the Sephardi religious party. To tackle it, he proposed the equilibration of tradition and progress, just as in the socioeconomic realm he bruited the equilibration of individual welfare and the interest of the collective. He offered no practical political way to bring tradition and progress into social and cultural equilibrium; instead, he settled for the claim that Israeli society is typified by disequilibrium between difficult intellectual and cultural questions and the lack of ways to cope with them.

The third value-related problem that Rotenstreich discusses stems from the Jewish–Arab military conflict and is related to the Israeli moral concept of "purity of arms" (*tohar ha-nesheq*, akin to "fighting clean"). The issue has accompanied the Yishuv and Israel in all their struggles, including the present-day armed conflict between Israel and the Palestinian Authority. Here again, Rotenstreich follows Ahad Ha'am's lead in this controversy and adheres to the humanistic moral doctrine that prompted Ahad Ha'am to issue a ringing public condemnation in the early 1920s after hearing a rumor about the killing of an Arab child by Jews.

Let us conclude this part of our introduction by saying that Rotenstreich offers Israeli society no unequivocal solution to its vacillation about the values of economic equality, cultural equilibrium, and human morality in the midst of a war that was forced on it. However, he regards the country's ceaseless vacillation about these issues as a moral stance that may provide Diaspora Jews with an example and, by so doing, add to Israel's political status in the Diaspora a spiritual dimension.

The foregoing led Rotenstreich to conclude that Zionism, as a national and cultural ideology that steers Klal Yisrael toward a collective goal, does not exist on the brink of the new millennium but must be renewed. Unlike Zionists who claim that Zionism has finished its historical role, which they deem to have been justified in its own time, Rotenstreich calls for the reformulation of the Zionist ideology so that it will be suited to the Jewish people's new situation and be able to provide a framework of ideology and values for its being a collective entity. He expresses the belief that the classical Zionist ideology has failed to provide an appropriate answer for this specific condition of being a collective entity and has focused on the creation of historical conditions for the establishment of this entity. He deems Ahad Ha'am's teachings to have become irrelevant, since a "problem of the Jews" in the Diaspora of the sort that Ahad Ha'am described no longer exists, and the "problem of Judaism," in its various manifestations, is unsolvable either in Israel or in the Diasporas. In lieu of these two historical questions, one may say that Rotenstreich confronts the "Jewish-people question"; that is, whether the Jews will continue to be a national entity—a question that preoccupied all modern Jewish national thinking from Simon Dubnow via Ahad Ha'am to the intellectuals of the Bund.

Thus, mindful of the situation, Rotenstreich proposed the reformulation of the Zionist ideology. He proposed that an important place in this reformulation be reserved for the existence of the Diaspora by inculcating a collective national consciousness linked to the State of Israel and by encouraging halutsic aliya, if not mass aliya. This mission statement led Rotenstreich back to the basic idea of the national center, but with a different emphasis. Ahad Ha'am believed that the spiritual center, the repository of Jewish values, would influence the Diaspora. Rotenstreich, in contrast, advocates the co-opting of the Diaspora into Israel's social and policy affairs in view of his *a priori* ideological premise that Israel is the state of the entire Jewish people. In this fashion, Rotenstreich hoped, Diaspora Jews would elect voluntarily and personally to be Israel's partners without making the country their permanent home. In turn, he expected Israel to decide to co-opt Diaspora Jewry into its life. Such a relationship, in his opinion, would create a Jewish national public domain of a new and different kind. It would create not a religious public, a persecuted people, or impoverished masses, but a free public that has chosen to exist in a multicultural national collective that transcends territory and politics. By so choosing, this free Jewish public will elect subjectively, on the basis of a collective will and ideological decision, to counteract the assimilative objective conditions. Thus, Rotenstreich's outlook is unquestionably anchored in voluntaristic principles and utopian leanings.

Notes

1. Mapai, the leading party in the Zionist Labor Movement in Palestine, was founded in 1930 and embraced most members of the movement except for Ha-Shomer ha-Tsa'ir and other small groups. In 1933, Mapai became the leading party in the Zionist Movement and the Yishuv (the Jewish community of preindependence Israel), led them in the process of establishing the State of Israel, and served as the ruling party until 1977. (During its tenure at the helm, it underwent metamorphoses, splittings, and mergers, and was renamed the Israel Labor Party.)

2. The small political group Min ha-Yesod ("From the Foundation") seceded from Mapai due to the dismissal of Pinchas Lavon as Secretary General of the Histadrut (the General Federation of Labor). Lavon was unseated in the course of a controversy about whether he had been responsible, while serving as Minister of Defense, for botched sabotage operations by Israeli intelligence in Egypt in 1954 and a

dispute over the succession to Ben-Gurion as head of the party and the state in the early 1960s.

3. N. Rotenstreich, "Socialism and the Problem of Responsibility," *Molad* 10:55, Oct.–Nov. 1952, pp. 18–25 (Hebrew).

4. See, for example, N. Rotenstreich, "Changes in Israel–Diaspora Relations (1974/75), in ibid., *Studies in Contemporary Zionism,* Jerusalem, 1977 (Hebrew, hereinafter: *Studies in Zionism*), pp. 33–44.

5. Op. cit., p. 38.

6. Ibid., "Zionism Today," in *Studies in Zionism,* pp. 48–49.

7. See, for example, N. Rotenstreich, [*Remarks*] *on the Renewal of the Zionist Idea,* Jerusalem, 1972, p. 19. See also N. Rotenstreich, [*Remarks*] *on Contemporary Jewish Existence,* Merhavia and Tel Aviv, 1972, pp. 139–162.

8. N. Rotenstreich, "Between the State of Israel and Zionism," in *Studies in Zionism,* pp. 64–66.

9. N. Rotenstreich, *Issues in Philosophy,* Tel Aviv, 1962 (Hebrew), Part II, Discussions about Marx, p. 219.

10. Ibid., p. 224; Karl Marx, "The Misery of Philosophy, a Response to P. Proudhon's Philosophy of Misery," quotation from Derek Sayer, *Readings from Karl Marx* (London: Routledge, 1989), p. 17.

11. N. Rotenstreich, "Israeli Society in Crisis," *Molad,* 1:31, October 1950, quoted from Rotenstreich, *Al ha-Temura,* pp. 152–161 (Hebrew).

12. This stance was the dominant one among the Mapai ideologues, nearly all of whom were rather extreme voluntarists and anti-determinists. Rotenstreich was a most profound representative of the dominant approach in the world of Mapai. Leaders such as Ben-Gurion and Lavon may also be considered pronounced voluntarists, in contradiction to their being no less people of authority.

13. This stance was widely held among Mapai ideologues. They were nearly all rather extreme ultra-voluntarists and anti-determinists.

14. N. Rotenstreich, "The First Pincer," *Molad,* 8:43, October–November 1951. Quoted from N. Rotenstreich, *Al ha-Temura,* pp. 162–169. The year 1951 is noted at the end of the article in the latter publication; this may denote the year the article was written.

15. N. Rotenstreich, "Social Trends in the State of Israel," *Bitsaron,* 26:6 (150), May 1952, pp. 77–85 (Hebrew), quoted from Rotenstreich, *Al ha-Temura,* pp. 170–177; ibid., "Technique and Politique," *Molad,* 9:52–53, August 1952, pp. 183–191 (Hebrew);

ibid., "Width and Height," *Ha-Doar,* 32:15, Feb. 20, 1953, pp. 285–286 (Hebrew).

16. See above for the definition of its main fundamental. One may say that *Mamlakhtiyut* corresponds, to some extent, to European republicanism.

17. Mapam. a Socialist Zionist party that had Marxist leanings and pro-Soviet sympathies, commanded a solid majority in the kibbutz movement. Established in 1948 by a group that seceded from Mapai in 1942–1944, members of the Ha-shomer ha-Tsa'ir movement, and smaller radical Socialist Zionist groups, it persevered in various metamorphoses until the 1980s.

18. Forty-six of the 120 members of the first elected Israeli parliament were members of Mapai and nineteen were members of Mapam. Generally, in Israel's first decade the two parties accounted for more or less half of the parliament (but only in the first parliament were they were more than half).

19. N. Rotenstreich, "Exploration of Concepts Relating to the Essence of the Jewish Exile," in Rotenstreich, *Al ha-Temura, Chapters on Issues of Nation and State,* Tel Aviv, 1953 (Hebrew).

20. N. Rotenstreich, "Parallel Tracks," op. cit., pp. 91–94.

21. N. Rotenstreich, "Testing the Spiritual-Center Idea," op. cit., pp. 95–108.

22. N. Rotenstreich., "Between a People and Its State," op. cit., pp. 109–118.

23. S. Rawidowicz, *Israel: The Ever-Dying People and Other Essays* (Sara F. Yoseloff Memorial Publications in Judaism and Jewish Affairs), Fairleigh Dickinson University Press, 1986.

24. "Israel and World Jewry 1962," *Congress Biweekly,* 1962.

25. N. Rotenstreich, "Changes in Israel-Diaspora Relations" (1975), in *Studies in Contemporary Zionism,* Jerusalem, 1977, pp. 38–43 (Hebrew).

26. "Exploration of an Issue—Exchange of Letters between D. Ben-Gurion and N. Rotenstreich," *Hazut* 3, Jerusalem, 1957, pp. 7–29 (Hebrew).

Chapter 1

Return and Modernity

The special relationship between the Jewish people and the Land of Israel was conceived in the traditional religious context as a relation based on promise, destiny and the overcoming of the exile. The first two components have a clear religious connection, referring as they do to the particular relation between the people and the divine. Promise can be understood as a kind of first step implied with that special relation, while destiny can be understood as pointing to the process and its future unfolding. On the other hand, exile can be understood as a historical, secular occurrence, since it was caused by war and the actions of the Roman Empire. In any event, the Jews' return to their ancestral home constituted a restoration on both historical and religious levels. From the point of view of the consciousness of the Jewish people, the religious and historical components form an integral unit. We shall refer, for instance, to Jeremiah (29:14): "I will turn away your captivity[. . .] and I will bring you again into the place whence I caused you to be carried away captive." We notice here that the historical situation of captivity is related to a suprahistorical cause, that is to say, divine intervention. The historical situation is characterized apodictically as "captivity," and the abolition of that woeful condition is regarded as a "return," effected by divine intervention, to "the place" from whence God himself had removed the People of Israel. Although promise and destiny are not explicitly mentioned in the passage from Jeremiah, we can nevertheless say that the stated dependence on a transcendental cause leaves us to consider the relationship between that cause and the dynamics of promise and destiny.

※ ※ ※

These remarks are intended to serve as a point of departure for an analysis of the notion of return set against the background of modernity. Few comments on modernity, in its broad sense, are necessary to shed light on the transformation of the concept of return. First of all, let us post modernity's opposition to what is often described as fundamentalism. That is, its rejection of the literalist adherence to ancient texts or to processes expressed in these texts or concepts. Modernity nurtures a concern with preserving trends and thus with changes that have occurred, and are occurring, in the course of history. The rejection of fundamentalism may be characterized as an attempt to regard historical processes in terms of their immanent nature. The modernist attitude regarding the natural process is of course a reflection of the modern understanding of nature and the approach to the study of nature, namely the scientific method. Here nature is understood as a sum-total of phenomena and not, for instance, as a manifestation of the divine presence, as interpreted in traditional religions. The essence of nature as knowledge of phenomena is not a description of the inner structure of nature, but that of the phenomena present, or in a sense visible. This trend of modern natural sciences displays a basic tendency to regard phenomena in their own immanent context and not to attempt to relate them to some primal origin or source beyond the phenomena as such. For the modernist approach, the interpretation of the mundane aspect of nature therefore becomes central.

It can thus be said that the reference to history as an immanent process in the world and not as an event grounded in transcendent causes is an extension of the modernist understanding of nature. Hence, modernity can be understood as an attempt to look at various spheres of reality from an immanent point of view. To underscore the significance of this point we may observe that a conception of nature and history as transcendent processes is an essential feature of traditional religions, including of course, Judaism. What is characteristic of the modern approach is the—explicit or implicit—separation between the phenomena and the transcendent context. Furthermore, in terms of the historical process, the modernist conception emphasizes the aspect of time and thus that of change. By and large, what goes by the term "secularism" is but an expression of that basic attitude.

To continue the description of the elements of modernity, society, and the state become prominent as, in a sense, self-contained entities. The idea of the social contract referring to agreement between human beings and not to divine legislation is a striking example of that shift characteristic of modernity. The notion of emancipation in the broad sense as the freeing of slaves, and in more limited sense as applying to the position of Jews in society and state, is grounded in that same trend of modernity. The limitation of society of state to the immanent context is only the other side of the separation between them and the context in which the religious affiliation of the state expresses the relation to transcendence. To sum up, we may say that the two aspects of modernity, that of separation from transcendence in the metaphysical and historical context and limitation to the immanent interaction between human beings, are relevant to an understanding of the idea of return in the texture of modernity.[1]

※ ※ ※

Thus, modernity brought about an articulation of those elements of return present in the traditional Jewish context, which can be understood as being akin to the immanent interpretation. They are, in the first place, the element of distance between the people and the land as well as of the dispersion of the people and their subjugation to other people or states. If subjugation is too strong a term, we can speak of dependence on other people. It can be said that distance and dispersion have a geographical or territorial meaning, which, as such, carries additional connotations, whereas subjugation or dependence already have a connotation of lack of sovereignty or of an inferior position within the sphere of relations between groups, or as compared with the position of other groups. It might be appropriate to mention here that a kind of premodern interpretation of the essence of the "Galut" (Exile) of the Jewish people can be found in the Maharal of Prague,[2] who said that every existing entity and mainly the human being is meant to be self-dependent. Galut is an impairment of that metaphysical principle since it, in a sense, degrades the position of man, equating it to that of an animal. Galut is a change in the order established by God. It departs from that order. Underlying that statement is an interpretation of the space or place as being specific to being in general and to human beings in particular. Human beings are meant to be self-supporting and their position is expressed in their occupation of an appropriate place. Place is not only a correlate of individual human beings, but also of collective entities.

Thus there is a "natural place" to which human beings are exposed. This premodern interpretation of the place, which is basically an Aristotelian interpretation, is the point of departure for a conception that brings together the relation between human beings and God who assigned to them the place on the one hand, and the naturalness of the place on the other.

In the traditional interpretation of place there is a negative evaluation of the actual place in which the people live, since the place is not the one assigned to the people—as we saw in Jeremiah. One of the basic trends of the modern interpretation of return is a closer analysis of the situation as it is, that is to say an analysis of the position in the present not only the way of comparing it with the past but by bringing to the fore the improprieties of the present situation. Return involves an analysis of the situation that is to be resolved by the return. This leads us to an emphasis on the sociological aspects of the situation and sometimes to what can be described as the sociological contraction of the interpretation of the Galut.

Before going into these components, we should note that one of the aspects of modernity—aspects also present in premodern trends—is the shift toward human acts as rooted in the Galut situation and intended to change it by means of return. We find an attempt of Simcha Luzzato's writings[3] to connect the position of the people in the Galut to the mode of its existence. People subjugated to a state are easily taken advantage of by it. They are compelled to serve the state, since they have no other choice. Thus the fact that Jews are concentrated in trade and commerce is one of the manifestations of their position of dependence on the surrounding societies and states. Indeed, Luzzato did not speak of the action to be undertaken in order to extract the Jewish people from that position, an attitude that we find again in the premodern trends, for example, in the precursors of religious Zionism.

In this trend, accordion to J.M. Pines, we find the formulation that it is necessary to shift the demand to reform the cult and the service to the reforms of life: the center of gravity is the reform of the society and its mode of life. This trend was summed up by M.J. Lilienblum when he said that what was needed was not a change in values but a change in our life in the Galut. We can sum up by saying that this first manifestation of modernity emphasizes the aspect of return by focusing on the day-to-day situation, which leads to return or should lead to it. The notion of return is present but the motivation toward it is meant to be placed in the present and not in the return as such with its direction toward the past. Return is an outcome and as such is not, at least not initially, a norm based in the past or echoing it. Return is a future situation to be brought about by action forming part of the rejection of the present.

※ ※ ※

The interaction between the notion of return and its position as a goal on the one hand and some aspects of modernity on the other can be formulated in the following way. As long as return remains a focal point, an analysis of the present situation is the case even when emphasis is laid not on coming back in the historical sense of the term, but rather on attributes of independent existence. To be sure, in as much as an analysis of the contemporary situation leads to the view that that situation tends toward universalism, which, as such, absorbs differences between collective entities and overcomes them, the correlate of that interpretation is the overcoming of the notion of return. Thus we can say that in the analysis of the contemporary situation the notion of return—whether directly or indirectly—is retained, whereas the concern with trends of a utopian character; for example, evident in the original Reform movement, brought about an annulment of the notion of return because of universalism conceived as the guiding trend of modern mankind.

※ ※ ※

We shall attempt now—in a typological approach—to present some of the major issues in terms of the contemporary situation, which focus on the gaps between Jewish existence and the surrounding world and thus turn again to the notion of return motivated by an analysis of the modern situation. First we refer to the aspect of race as it is presented in Moses Hess's *Rome and Jerusalem*: Hess rather poignantly says that the Germans do not hate the religion of the Jews the way they hate the Jewish race.[4] It is obvious that the shift from the historical religious background to the aspect of race or descent in the biological connotation, is meant to emphasize the limitations of the impact of the historical process, that process which occupies Hess's early writings and is the most prominent element of the system. The emphasis on the racial aspect leads to the conclusion that there are limitations to the harmonistic trend of the historical process. This has to be said precisely because Hess concurrently adheres to the idea or ideal of the unity of mankind, though its realization calls, as a prerequisite for the establishment of the position of the Jewish people. Thus the harmonious aspect of mankind appears to be coexistent with the aspect of the differences between nations, which cannot be erased.

Hess uses the term "race" though the term is not unambiguous. This was the case in the literature of the eighteenth and nineteenth centuries, which employed that term. To be sure, the biological component is present in these discussions, stressing the common descent of a distinct ethical entity, but we notice also that the term "race" appears in the context of humanity as the human race, though it is obvious that the component of the ethnical entity cannot be attributed to that meaning. We find in the literature that probably influenced Hess—a conjunction of the aspect of common descent with that which points to a civil role or the conjunction between descent and the soul of the people, that is, its spirit or genius. We have to recall that the biological component is present also in the term natio and in this case, it is even more prominent because we can easily trace the root of the term to nasci. What Hess apparently wanted to present is the constant existence of the ethnical entity, referring to the Jewish people as manifesting a common descent and a continuous collective entity, which has to be related to the process of history in the nineteenth century.

Let us look now at a different presentation of this situation of antagonism between the collective entity of the Jews and the surrounding world. It should be mentioned parenthetically in this context that the term anti-Semitism is a modern term, emerging in the nineteenth century.

⁂ ⁂ ⁂

When Leo Pinsker[5] analyzed the collective situation of the Jews, he referred to collective xenophobia, which, as such, is obviously a general concept applicable to collective existences in general. He even uses the term "Platonic hatred." At the same time Pinsker emphasizes a possibly unique feature of the Jewish situation within the non-Jewish world: the Jews are conceived of as ghosts, that is to say, beings wandering around in the world and eliciting fear. This is so because the Jews somehow embody a past existence that has vanished but they are still visible in the present. Precisely this application of semi-psychological descriptions is relevant in this context because as is well-known, traditional Christianity considered the Jews to belong to the past because Judaism had been replaced by Christianity. To some extent, the Jews did not follow that rhythm of history that prescribed their disappearance.

Pinsker shifted the Christian evaluation of the Jews to a sociological context, emphasizing the permanent quality of the clash between the Jews and the surrounding world. In as much as the shift occurred from the theological judgment of the Jews to a psychosociological analysis of their position, the gap between the Jews and the environment ceased to be ideological and became psychological. In this sense it is apparently more enduring as a description of the clash. At this point we could say that the precondition for return is an analysis of the situation that will lead to the removal of the Jewish presence from the existing surroundings, that is, from the non-Jewish world.

An additional feature comes to the fore in the context of this supposed change in the situation of the Jews as characterized in the notion of emancipation and its transference to the Jewish context. Concurrently with discernment of the permanent features of Jewish existence, skepticism emerged vis-à-vis emancipation either as an expression of disappointment, or as a disbelief in terms of the validity and effect of the equal rights to be granted to the Jews. Hatred of the Jews as analyzed by Herzl points precisely to the disappointment vis-à-vis emancipation.[6] That disillusion can refer either to the slow process of emancipation or to the preeminence of hatred, since national existence is but an epiphenomenon of hatred, or else, more empirically—the situation of the exile is essentially a situation of permanent crisis. Any crisis in the surrounding world, for example, the Dreyfus Affair, had an impact on the situation of the Jews. It should be pointed out that the concern with the present day situation does not necessarily preclude the expectation of at least a mitigation of it in the future, and indeed Zionists have been involved since the beginning of the twentieth century in searching in the present for the source of the future, to achieve a mitigation of the present predicament. Yet one of the aspects of modernity is—against all expectations of the remote future—awareness of the pressures of the present day situations. Here, modernity has been interpreted differently, that is to say, concern with reality overshadows the expectation of the goal of history. Here, too, we can define this correlation between the analysis of the situation and the notion of return, that is, that the more the situation is essentially a critical one, the more the adherence to return becomes central as the only way out of the predicament of the situation and its pressures.

※ ※ ※

In order to emphasize an additional feature of the contemporary situation we shall describe—not the clash between the Jews and the surrounding world—but the impact of the surrounding world on Jewish behavior and the modes of life of the Jewish people. As a general heading of this mode of relation between the Jews and the outside world we can suggest the term: contraction. Jewish existence was contracted both economically and culturally—and we combine two different analyses of the Jewish situation under one heading. The central aspect in the economic analysis, which is the other side of the coin of contraction, is that the Jews did not participate professionally in the full range of economic activities. Their modes of economic subsistence were confined to several and only few directions and thus are described as being nonproductive. Hence the return is meant to be a move from contraction to breadth, as it went under the term—"productivization." The underlying notion seems to be that only an independent national existence lends itself to a full range of economic activity and at this point the national and political normalcy and the economic one appear to be intertwined. Though return as such does not historically have the connotation of productivization it is turned into a basis for it.

The second expression of contraction is the danger of the abolition of the national existence including the unity of the Jewish people. The hard core of contraction is the exposure of Jewish creativity to the overwhelming influence of the outside world. That influence negates the possibility of preserving the cultural and spiritual independence of the Jewish people and the cultivation of that independence. This is the central point in Ahad Ha'am's interpretation,[7] who emphasized that as a result of the removal from the Land of Israel, the national "ego" of the Jewish people does not embrace the whole scope of the individual "ego" or the person as an individual belonging to the Jewish people. The contraction of the influence of the "ego" is due to the lack of essential conditions for that impact, that is to say that the exposure of the Jews to the outside world is concomitant with the lack of conditions for one national existence. Hence the problem facing the Jews—what is described as the tragic fate—is to preserve the separate existence as a people within the process of the participation in the general culture. Thus the aim is to lift up the clash between the two trends to a level of a synthesis.

Thus we can sum up by saying that an analysis of the present situation in terms of the clash between the position of the Jews underlying the background of return, brings about an emphasis on the political, social, economic, and cultural aspects of that clash. Dialectically the absorption of the impact does not overshadow the aspects of clash, though different ideologies concentrate on different aspects. A synopsis of these ideologies brings about the broad spectrum of the aspects of the contemporary Jewish situation within the structure of the modern world. To be sure, in terms of the analysis the idea of return is an idea within a content of a background, whereas in terms of the application of the national ideology in the modern sense to the Jewish existence the idea of return becomes an explicit notion. We can now turn to this last aspect of our exploration.

※ ※ ※

Structurally speaking a distinction can be made between the analytical aspect of the problem of Jewish nationhood in the context of modernity and the ideological aspect related to it. The two aspects are correlated but the idea of return becomes prominent more within the context of the ideological approach than within the context of the analytical one. Analytically, to come back to this description, the idea of return looms in the background of the exploration and exposition of the situation of the Jews, whereas that exploration takes advantage of some conceptual tools present in the vocabulary of the modern approach to social existence. Inasmuch as the analytical approach makes central the element of strangeness between the Jews and their environment along with the various manifestations of that strangeness. The idea of return motivates the analytical approach toward greater awareness of the impact of strangeness on return or—from the other end, since return did not take place, strangeness is the most prominent element of the situation as it is. The ideological approach makes the idea of return an explicit component of the horizon of aspirations of the Jewish people.

This has to be said in spite of the Uganda controversy.[8] In that controversy a kind of distinction became prominent, between the "here and now" solution of the predicament of the Jews and the solution of the national problem of the Jewish people in its various components. As it is known, that controversy even absorbed the previously noted distinction between levels of the messianic realization, that is to say, that insofar as the Messiah the son of Joseph is concerned there is no necessity to assume the realization of return, which amounts to a return to the Land of Israel, and not any digression, that is, Uganda. The overwhelming historical fact is that these distinctions have not been accepted, let alone incorporated into the structure of the Jewish national aspiration. Return remained the focus of the solution either of the predicament of the Jews or that of Judaism or of both.

This point has to be emphasized because the adherence to the idea of return makes Jewish national aspirations somehow unique. This is even more so since there is no question about it that the Jewish national ideology absorbed and incorporated some of the basic notions of the European national ideology.

※ ※ ※

In the first place we have to notice that the Jewish population entertaining national aspirations is not a native population; that is to say, a population that lives in a certain area and aspires to express its existence in a framework of statehood or through the agency of self-government. If we look, for example, into a statement characteristic of Italian nationalism—we find the emphasis is laid on the nationalities that do not possess a government issuing from their innermost life. These nationalities are subject to compulsion imposed on them from outside. They have become the means for others' purposes and therefore are mere objects. The distinction between the position of the subject and that of the object, that is, the distinction between the governing authority and the subjugated people, is echoed in Herzl's distinction between the aspired position of the Jews as a subject and the given position as an object. Yet the object in the Italian context connotes subjugation and thus a distinction between the people and the government or state. The position of an object in the Jewish context is more comprehensive because it encompasses the difference between the environment and the Jews and not only the difference between the population and the governing body. Thus the very discernment of the features of being an object contains in itself the discrepancy between what should be the position of the Jews in the broad sense of the term, and their actual position. Hence the notion of return leads to the enlargement of the analysis and that in turn leads to a different direction of the analytical basis underlying the ideological aspirations. If a national ideology is meant to present a people's aspirations related to its actual situation, we find that the Jewish national ideology does not present only the attempt to actualize Jewish self-government as a manifestation of Jewish independence. It is bound to go a step deeper, to put it like that, that is to say, to establish a territorial basis and a social comprehensiveness that would find their eventual manifestation in government "issuing from the innermost life." Return becomes therefore both a goal and a precondition for the territorial and social ingathering, which is turn are the preconditions for the embodiment in government.

From the analytical point of view strangeness is discerned as a situation and as a manifestation of the lack of basis for existence, which is considered to be the adequate basis of the Jewish people: from the ideological point of view the return becomes an explicit idea pointing to the goal, the achievement of which is the condition sine qua non of the national independence and its manifestations.

We conclude that the ideology of the Jewish national movement exhibits actually the particular situation of the Jewish people, both from the point of view of its aspirations as well as that of its existence. Though the Jewish ideological formulation is in a sense of variation in the general trend of nationalism, the transformation of the concept of the national ideology could not eliminate the particularities of Jewish existence. In this sense the Jewish national aspirations belong to the scope of modern nationalism but as the same time make prominent the unique position of the Jewish people. The notion of return is a focus of that unique position. Without going into problems of the contemporary situation, which is modern even when it is postmodern, we have to come to the conclusion that the particularities of Jewish nationalism did not disappear. On the contrary, the clashes between Jewish nationalism and Arab aspirations, the position of the State of Israel as a state of its society and of the Jewish people, the coexistence of the problem of the Jews and the presence of the state—all these are illustrations of this complex situation: Jews dwell in modernity but the particular features of their existence did not disappear with modernity or because of it. Some aspects of this situation will be our concern presently.[9]

Notes

1. There is a vast literature on the structure of modernity and its trend. Because of the comprehensive character of the book we refer to Jürgen Habermas, *The Philosophical Discourse of Modernity: Twelve Lectures*, transl. by Frederick Lawrence. Foliberg Press, Cambridge, 1967.

2. Judah Loew ben Becalel, known as the Maharal of Prague, took the position that there exists a natural order. The situation of the Galut is a deviation from that order. He is the author of many books.

3. Simcha-Simone Luzzato analyzed the situation of the Jews in the city of Venetia during the Renaissance period, emphasizing their professions, including their shortcomings.

4. Hess's book: *Rome und Jerusalem, die letzte Nationalitatfrage* is significant in its title and subtitle as well. *Rome und Jerusalem* points to the historical antithesis between Rome and the Jews but also to the contemporary development of the unification of Italy. Hence the subtitle presents the Jews' national position as the last national question of the world once the Italian question or problem was possibly solved.

5. Pinsker, Leo (Yudah Leib). His book: *Auto-emancipation* was published in German in 1882. Pinsker coined the term auto-emancipation as self-delivery against the concept of emancipation, which connotes a granting of rights from the external authority. The book was published anonymously.

6. Herzl's stay in Paris evoked his interest, and concern, with the growing anti-Semitism. The Dreyfus case was a turning point in his development. His book: *Der Judenstaat* (The Jewish State, 1896) suggests a solution for the Jewish question, that is, the plight of Jewish existence as strangers, or the "Ultimate Others," in the countries in which they live.

7. Ahad Ha'am expressed his conceptions in essays and articles. There is no single book that summarizes his ideas. The articles are contained in his four volumes. A selection, translated by L. Simons, is available.

8. The reference is to the proposal to settle Jews in Uganda (1903). Herzl negotiated this idea with the British Government in the attempt to bring about a solution to the unsafe situation of the Jews, in particular in the Russian empire, by way of emigration to a semi-autonomous region. In 1903 the Zionist Congress debated the proposal and it was finally rejected in 1907. Herzl died in 1904. The Zionist Congress resolves at the same time that the Zionist Movement was entitled to initiate settlements in the Land of Israel.

9. Some references are to historical books:

a) Adolf Bohm's book *Die Zionistische Bewegung*, two-volume. 1936–1937, is a very comprehensive study of the history of Zionism. The limit is indicated by the dates of publication.

b) Arthur Herzberg: *The Zionist Idea: A Historical Reader.* Temple Books, 1969, several editions.

c) Martin Buber. *On Zion: The History of an idea*, with a forward by Nahum N. Glazer: transl. by Stanley Godman. London, East and West Library, 1973.

(The original publication Israel and Palestine, the history of an idea)

(d) Jacob Katz: *Jewish Emancipation and Self Emanicipation.* The Jewish Publication Society, Philadelphia, 1980.

Chapter 2

Activity and the Present

Zionism, both as an ideological setting and as a movement, brought about the existence of the State of Israel. Every national movement is ideological, since it aspires to establish a political framework, taking the shape of the state, which in turn is meant to be an organized manifestation of a national aspiration: a social aspiration is, by definition, aimed at an ideological goal. If this is to be applied to national movements in general, it applies even more so to the Jewish people and its national movement. National movements, by and large, are manifestations of people dwelling in their own lands: as such, they attempt to reach the political manifestation of their existence, which will express and enhance it.

The factual reality of the Jewish people was different: its national movement was not a movement of liberation, but one of return, which was our theme in the previous chapter. As such, it aimed at the creation of the population basis of statehood, that is to say, to lay the groundwork for the synthesis of the demographic and territorial aspects of existence. The concept of return in a nutshell is the specific manifestation of the peculiar character of the Jewish national movement. This is so in spite of the many problematic aspects related to that goal, from the internal Jewish point of view, as well as from the point of view of the conflict with the Arab world.

At the outset, we must distinguish the modern character of Zionism—and the longing to come back to Zion, obviously an essential part of the traditional horizon of the Jewish people, that is, the conjunction between the religious and national attitudes.

In limiting to some extent the broad notion of modernity—to come back to that trend[1] we shall emphasize two components in our attempt to isolate the conceptual background of Zionism. The comprehensive process of "modernization" in which different elements are selected from the spectrum of tradition and interpreted as part of contemporary change, constitutes an innovation that focuses on a new approach to both nature and history. History is not viewed as a permanent reservoir, but as a sum total of temporal aspects, where temporality is a different meaning, including that which is flowing or changing. Several components of modern historical consciousness bring to the fore the changes that are characteristic of the process and its results, as opposed to that which is permanent, or that which, as tradition, has been understood as immune to change and above it.

If we look at this shift in perspective and at its significance in the Jewish context, we could say that in the nineteenth century we notice needs of a shift from looking at tradition as a progress of accumulation to interpreting it from the point of view of selection. From the broad reservoir of tradition, shaped by the accumulative process, several elements are selected. These are meant to be the point of departure for the aspirations in the contemporary sense of the term, and concurrently, they are conceived as congruous with the trend of time.

※ ※ ※

Zionism is part of that shift both in terms of the background and in terms of its explication.

An aliment of secular "modernization" is the concept of emancipation, originally implying the liberation of certain spheres of reality from subjection, as, for instance, the emancipation of the state from the rule of the church. In another context, emancipation connotes the liberation of slaves, etc. The state is seen as grounded in a contract, as some thinkers thought, and not in divine legislation. It can be viewed as free from dependence on religion, either dogmatically or ecclesiastionally, the state becomes an immanent mode of human existence, and thus, as a matter of principle, open to the rule of law.

These three aspects—secularity, emancipation, and the state based on the rule of law—are of particular significance for modern Judaism, and for the possibility of asserting and formulating Jewish goals. The various settings of Jewish existence throughout the ages were of a religious or ecclesiastic character. This applies both to the relation with Christianity and with Islam, though from the point of view of modernity, the relation to the former is more pertinent. Within the religious framework, the Jews could not be conceived as belonging to their surrounding society; the maximum they could achieve was a kind of "give" and "take" between themselves and their environment. Within the new opening characterized by the three components mentioned above, there was a real, or at least open potential for the Jews to argue that they had a position within a structure based on secularity, emancipation, and the rule of law, or at least they were entitled to aspire to a position within that structure and expect a positive response from it. If the process was not essentially immersed in tradition, but related to secularity, the Jews could detach themselves from their tradition, at least to some extent, and demand the same from the environment. If the period was characterized by liberation from the rule of the Church, or positively by the rule of law, determining norms of behavior, the new perspective of being citizens opened the door to the Jews, the same door that had been closed when the person was not viewed as a citizen, but essentially as a believer or member of the Church. The new social and political setup was understood as a norm for the environment and as an opportunity for the Jews to obliterate, eventually, the difference or the distinction between the two traditions. The universal norm would be binding on the previous participants in the historical confrontation.

※ ※ ※

What is the relation between these trends of modernity and the basis of Zionism? Since we have already referred to the broad concept of emancipation, we can begin by recalling that Jews were granted emancipation in the Napoleonic period in France, or aspired to achieve it in the German state, by referring to the law—to the Rechtsstaat. They tried to assure their position in secular states, no longer conceived of as Christian. The Jews who addressed themselves to the new structure of the state were grounded in a religion, that is to say, a people belonging to a historically shaped collective. The emancipation granted or to be granted them, was intended essentially to the individual status. Why did this happen?

As long as Jews were conceived and perceived as a collective, they were viewed as a historical collective characterized by the religious character of their existence. In order to strike roots within the context of modernity they had to change the profile of tradition. The major or axial change has been the shift from collective to individual existence. They thought this change congruous with the character of the modern state, and by the same token, instrument for their aspiration. The attempt to achieve the status of emancipation has been seen from outside and inside the Jewish realm, as conforming to the change in European history.

The affiliation of individuals with a religion in the sense of articles of faith and of an organized community was conceived as being outside the sphere or the aspiration since the religious affiliation was now seen as characteristic of certain individuals and not of human beings in the universal sense. The overcoming of particularity was both a response to the character of the commonwealth as well as precondition for joining it. Zionism, paradoxically, was related to the modern trends, but at the same time placed the emphasis on Jewish collective existence and not on that of individual Jews.

Zionism became a concrete aspiration within the historical context. It did not rely on the goal of return in the messianic sense of that term, but selected from the sum total of the components of tradition the element of collective existence, dimly relevant to the present, too, but seen as calling for an essential condition of it, namely the territorial basis. That basis is identical with Zion, or the Land of Israel. Both have been translated into the structure of political entities in terms of the integration of the territorial basis and the political reality expressed in statehood.

With all due differences, the same change or reemphasis applies to the position of the Hebrew language, reserved over the ages as a language of the tradition, or as a medium for prayers and texts. Against the modern background, the Hebrew language was conceived as one of the manifestations of the collective existence of the Jews, that is, a medium of communication in the present and thus epitomizing the shift from the written Scriptures to the spoken medium.

Hence, the relation of Zionism to modern reality is to be found in the acceptance of the principle of nationalism or nationality as justifying the effort of the Jews and their aspiration.[2] Because of the status of the people in Jewish religious awareness and tradition, Zionism could transfer the assertion of the people to its own context. The difference between the traditional interpretation of the position of the people and the modern one is that the former stressed the people as recipients of divine revelation, while the latter stressed the status of a collective entity according to the principle of existence.

A significant explication of this trend is expressed in the subtitle of Hess's book *Rome and Jerusalem: The Last Question of Nationality.*[3] The book deals with the historical process from different angles. In a sense it sees history from a universal point of view. Hess still maintains his affinity to the school he left behind, namely, socialism and the German philosophical trend. But he argues that after the unity of Italy became a historical fact only one national problem remained without a solution—the position of the Jewish people within the process of history. In short, if history is involved in the trend of realization of national aspirations, and that trend is characteristic of history in the universal sense, there is an obligation to bring about the realization of the national aspiration of the Jewish people.

※ ※ ※

What is the constitutive factor of the people, that is to say, is it a mere aspiration, or is it already an existing people whose national aspiration is but one of the manifestations of its existence? The shift to the historical process would be an actualization, but it could be interpreted also as establishing the national entity, at least in the sense of a contemporary existence.

In this context, Zionism is related to what Gershom Scholem described as coming back to history. This is not a "coming back" in the totalistic or messianic sense, because from that angle, of course, there is no need to come back to history: we are in it from the start. It is a return to history as a particular synthesis between meaning and time, by way of putting forward the existence in time, and by way of shaping factors meant to safeguard a continuous existence in time.

An additional characteristic feature emerges in this context in terms of the relation between the Jews and their environment. To employ here terms used by Herzl, we can say that the attempt is made to transform the object of emancipation into its subject. Emancipation will not be granted by external factors or authorities, including the state based on the rule of law. It will be achieved through the collective historical effort of these who seek it. Hence, the notion of auto-emancipation with the emphasis both on auto and emancipation, emerges, since the subject of emancipation will build it and be built by it.

These interrelated trends enable us to point to an additional feature of Zionism it is an ideological setting built to a large extent on an analysis of the reality that it emerged in and that it attempts to restructure. We find not a mere vision, but a conjunction of the element of aspiration and that of critique and analysis. The disappointment related to emancipation is of major significance in this texture, since it is the central issue of critique and analysis.

The parallel aspect of what we are analyzing is anti-Semitism. We must recall that "anti-Semitism" is a modern term: it emerged in the 1870s,[4] probably in order to make prominent the basic fact that Jews are rejected not only, or mainly, because of elements of religious tradition, but because of other factors, part of the modern world. This shift is made explicit in the various publications related to the emergence of anti-Semitism. Zionism referred to that issue by analyzing it, and by attempting to arrive at operational consequences. We have to mention the Dreyfus trial and its significance, for instance, for Herzl. To sum up we may say that we encounter the parallel two trends characteristic of Zionism, that is, the retreat from the environment of the non-Jewish world, and the attempt to strike roots in the concrete and real world. This is not a negation of the real world by way of an apocalyptic vision: it is not a retreat to the universalism of the Reform movement or one to the "four corners" of the ghetto. It is a retreat to the realm of the Jewish people, not in order to remove it from the historical reality, but in order to enable it to find its place within that reality.

※ ※ ※

What has become of the attempt to achieve normality,[5] as characterized in the Zionist idiom? Normality, in the various fields of its application has two meanings: one is that which exists according to a "norm," and the second is that which is frequent, accepted, or regular. When we deal with the normality of the Jewish people, we assume that the norm of the collective existence for the Jewish people is that of an independent existence characterized by the usual attributers—land, language, culture, state, etc. At the same time, we refer to what can be described as a statistical understanding of normality—that which is the common pattern of human existence. The Jewish people has to find its place in reality as it is shaped by that pattern.

The adoption of the notion of normality points to the two symmetrical trends characteristic of Zionism, namely acceptance of the pattern pertaining in the world, and its translation into Jewish existence. Hence Zionism as a phenomenon of modernity can be characterized by the fact that it converted elements of the Jewish tradition into dynamic components of modern historical reality. The emphasis on normalcy can be seen as a change and that change, in turn, is the other facet of the activity characteristic of Zionism.

Even the forerunners of religious Zionism emphasized the right to activity here and now, in spite of their messianic expectations. Hence it is not by chance that major religious Zionist thinkers made or applied the traditional distinction, between the Messiah the Son of David, with the eschatological connotation, and the Mesiah the Son of Joseph, with the possible application here and now. The activity of the Messiah the Son of Joseph does not replace the future coming of the Messiah the Son of David: it is a preparation for it. In this sense, we discern echoes of the modern situation even within the traditional religious context: auto-emancipation not only replaces emancipation, but makes the actions of people here and now the most prominent issue. The religious thinkers drew from traditional texts, finding in them a possible direction in the present.

The impact of modernity on the basic trend of Zionism can be seen in terms of the two components—the territorial basis and the common language as articulation and by the same token, activation. The two components were always present in Jewish tradition and in the historical awareness of the Jewish people. Modernity gave them significance as norms and aims within the horizon of present activity, adopting the orientation characteristic of modern national movements leading to activity within the situation as it is.

In terms of a third component, not characteristic of Zionism as such but only of a particular ideological trend that emerged within it, we find a different structure. This is what goes by the name of Socialist Zionism,[6] which we mention here not from the point of view of its essence, but as an additional expression of the impact of modernity. This ideological orientation and its concrete manifestations cannot be considered as an explication or articulation of the past but as a deliberate innovation. It is not an activation but an attempt at a synthesis, that is to say, an attempt to bring together the national movement characteristic of the ideology and the movement of the nineteenth century, with its orientation toward shaping the structure of the society to be established in the process of return. The difference between articulation and integration becomes evident when we consider the various attempts to find a basis for the synthesis in the prophetic legacy of Judaism, let alone in the analysis of the socioeconomic conditions of the Jewish people in the surrounding environments. We can consider this trend toward a synthesis as an additional manifestation of the relation of Zionism to modernity, while remaining aware of the difference between the various components mentioned in this analysis.[7]

We are not attempting to present a full picture of the relation between the background of modernity and Zionism as an ideology and as a movement, but rather to show it as a major factor in the establishment of the State of Israel. Trends are not synonymous with reality and its various components. A prominent case in point is religious Zionism and its position within the context of our discussion, with reference to the interpretation of the messianic expectation. We can look at religious Zionism from a broader point of view, mainly from the perspective of discerning a trend that does not acknowledge modernity, though it may take advantage of it, for instance, to reach the goal of observing commandments traditionally dependent on a living presence in the Land of Israel.

Hence the exodus from the Diaspora and the return are understood as a precondition for the realization of the full scope of the commandments, and not as the realization of trends inherent in modernity. Involvement in the Zionist movement is then seen either as a fulfillment of the commandments or as a precondition for them. At the same time religious Jews in their various orientations were opposed to Zionism and are still opposed to it, even if some of them have adjusted themselves de facto to the existence of the State. It has to be added that not only Orthodox trends were opposed to Zionism, but also Reform Judaism, not because of the clash between the immanent and human realizations of national aspirations but because of its own universalistic orientation. Return to the Land of Israel and participation in national movements were conceived, and rightly so, as expressions of a particularistic orientation, and as such, opposed to universalism. Broadly speaking, the religious tradition in its various components has been a basis for the rejection of Zionism, whereas religious Zionism took advantage of the Zionist orientation and interpreted it to suit its own goals.

These various processes and trends were not fully articulated in the background that we are analyzing. Zionism as an ideology brought about a movement, and the movement attempted to materialize a goal centered around the notion of return. As we said above, Zionism always stressed the territorial factor—the Land of Israel—and the factor of language—

Hebrew. The separation of the territorial component led, to mention this again, as a matter of fact, to the Uganda controversy, that is to say, to the distinction between the territorial basis and the Land of Israel.

When we turn to the reality that took shape against the background of Zionism, we should emphasize, first, that the trend toward modernization has become even stronger in the course of recent decades, since the effect of science and technology in forming a comprehensive climate of opinion was not as powerful in the nineteenth century as it is now. In addition, realistic needs have led to additional involvement and active participation in modern civilization. The State of Israel thus strives continuously to take advantage of technological development and what goes with it. Involvement in a civilization of such strength and influence cannot be an isolated factor. It becomes and is a component of present-day reality in its various perspectives. Hence the impact of modernity did not weaken, but on the contrary, became even more palpable.

Yet, against this trend, we must remain aware of what can be described as the dialectic of return, for return, as an essential component of Zionism, cannot be exhausted in the geographic dimension only. The return brought about processes of encounter with the land, and the land is a context of associative meanings, both chronological and immediate. One of the manifestations of that process is the enduring interest, both scholarly and cultural, in the broad sense in the history of the Land of Israel. That dimension of the past has become prominent in itself, and not always as integrated into the broad context of the history of the Jewish people.

The discovery of the relics of the past is not confined to archaeology. It opens the door toward an attempt to understand various substantive aspects of the background of the present era in the Bible and in biblical research. This interest, again, is not confined to scholars. It led to a new or semi-new orientation regarding the position of the Bible as a source of the spiritual world of the Jewish people without forgetting the relation between the origin or source and that which followed it, that is to say, the relation between the Bible and the exegetic creativity of Judaism in the post-biblical period.

The return to the Hebrew language[8] accounts for the fact that the language of the past became the contemporary one. As such it ceased to be the medium only of prayer or of the written interpretation of Judaism, and became the medium of the communication, which is a modern phenomenon. Concern with the Bible becomes akin to the metamorphosis of the biblical language into the language of the present. Hence we can sum up: against the background of modernity, emergence of the consciousness of the relation between the present and the past has become a central topic of cultural orientation and creativity. The process characterized here can be understood as one leading to return not only in the territorial and linguistic sense, but also in the broader cultural one. That return does not mean the ignoring of the present era but a continuous re-interpretation of the relation between the present and the past.

※ ※ ※

There is another factor in contemporary Jewish reality that is not related to the situation of the State of Israel, but to that of Jewry living outside Israel, specifically in the Western world. Modernity in the Jewish context implied among other things the goal of emancipation and the disappointment of the Jews vis-à-vis, that is to say, vis-à-vis their position within European sociopolitical reality. But the historical process brought about a major territorial change: the center of gravity of the life of Diaspora Jews shifted from Europe to the United States. Here the emancipation of the Jews became an everyday reality above and beyond what Jews in Europe ever dreamed of. Hence emancipation became a reality far outrunning nineteenth-century ideology.

The realization of that process leading to Jewish integration in the Western world, that is, in the societies and cultures of their environment became a process parallel to the establishment of the State of Israel. One may say that the parallel process of emancipation and auto-emancipation "coexist" and should not be seen historically as displacing each other, as the advocates of auto-emancipation believed. We encounter modernity not only as a background, but also as a content, once we remain within the boundaries of description and analysis. This, in turn, is a major feature of the Jewish reality in the present era and, probably by the same token, a major problem of that reality. For the Zionist ideology, this has to be a point of departure for a reformulation of its orientation—but that issue lies beyond the scope of our analysis. We shall come back to that issue in the last chapter.

In any case, "return" as a phenomenon of modernity manifests itself as an attempt at renaissance. Modernity and renaissance are not synonyms. The question is how and to what extent they reinforce each other.

Notes

1. We refer again to Habermas's book mentioned in chapter 1.

2. Johann Huisinga: *Patriotism and Nationalism in European History*, pp. 97 ff. The Renaissance, pp. 243 ff. incl. in *Men and Ideas*, transl. by James S. Holmes and Hans van Marie. Princeton University Press, 1984.

3. See chapter 1.

4. The term was coined by W. Marr in Germany. On the issue, consult: A. Bein: Der neue Antisemitism and seine Bedeutung fur die Judenfrage. *Vierteljahresschrift fur Zeitgeschichte*, 1958, 340 ff.

5. Consult: J. Frankel: *Socialism and Jewish Nationsalism in Russia,* Cambridge University Press, 1961.

6. On normality in the social context, consult: Emile Durkheim: The Science of Normality 105 ff in his *Selected Writings*, transl. by Anthony Giddens. Cambridge University Press, 1972.

7. Among the later texts: Viktor Arlosoroff: *Der Judische Volkssocialismus,* Berlin 1919 is prominent.

8. The magazine *Ariel*, vol. 26 contains different analyses of the process of turning the Hebrew language from the language of the Scriptures into a language of everyday activization.

Chapter 3

Aspects of Renaissance

In chapter 1 we dealt with the notion of return, identifying it as one of the essential components of modern Zionism. In this context, return may have the topographical or geographical connotation of coming back to the land, specifically to the Land of Israel. Relation to land as part of space is a constant component of human or historical behavior, though the term "coming back" cannot make us oblivious to the roots of that process within the present-day situation, implying time and not space. The possible variations on the prefix "re" will occupy the next part of our analysis.

※ ※ ※

In employing the term renaissance we must distinguish its different components, remaining aware of the terminological aspect: the use of the term suggests the transmission of a notion from modern European history, mainly Italian, to the Jewish context.[1] Renaissance is terminologically and etymologically related to the Latin *renatus*, that is to say, born again or born anew. Originally it had the connotation of an intellectual adherence to the resources of classical or Greek culture, starting anew by criticizing the immediate past—the Middle Ages—and attempting to establish the influence of classical culture. Renaissance thus came to connote the revival of certain channels of activity or creativity, such as art or thought. When the notion is brought into the context of historical development in general and of the Jewish people in particular, it is no longer confined to certain channels of creativity. It is meant to express the general spectrum of activities, rooted in the infrastructure of the

Jewish people. Hence, we must first define some aspects of the notion of renaissance within the context of Jewish history.

The first component to be dealt with here can be defined as a rejuvenation, establishing a new vitality of Jewish creativity, not in this or that particular direction but in the broad sources of that creativity. In this context one could suggest an analogy between renaissance and revitalization. The question immediately arises whether revitalization is related to return or whether it is vitalization and the prefix *re* points only to the historical succession: that is to say there have been previous periods of Jewish vitality and a new one is about to begin. This notion should be seen as related to contact with the basis of the real human life. Because of the emphasis on real life, this element of renaissance can be understood as openness to various aspects of the impact of present-day reality. We notice that very often use of the prefix *re* points to the possibility that what is considered to be new may in fact contain existing elements. Without examining in detail each and every interpretation of the Jewish national movement in the modern era, we can say that one of the most prominent interpreters of the renaissance trend was the writer and thinker Micha Joseph Berdichevsky.[2] He advocated involvement of the Jewish people in their environment, and emphasized this point to the extent of finding a contradiction between relating to concrete existence and returning to the sources. He considered the past as impoverishing creativity or at least hindering it. The second component in the concept of renaissance is of a more defined character, connoting the revitalization of the past. One could suggest that this component is more frequently present in the context of Zionism, since Zionism essentially connotes, as we have seen, a return, not only to the land as a spatial basis of existence, but also—strikingly—to the Hebrew language. The language of writing became a spoken one with all the levels of speech that go with it. The complicated interaction between the language of written sources, including the Scriptures, and everyday usage emerged as one of the features of the revitalization. These two components do not exhaust the range of return to the people's roots of creativity. Precisely in this context, for instance, the educational direction in Zionism gave an impetus to the teaching of the Bible in the school curriculum. The Bible has always been considered as the most important manifestation, or even the basis, of the Jewish people and its creativity. Because of the emphasis on the position of the Bible as the basis, and the first link in the succession of Jewish interpretations over the ages, we cannot define the first stage of renewed Jewish creativity as secularist. There is no need to emphasize that the Bible was always regarded as a divine document. Considering the later interpretations as secondary is only the complementary aspect of the return to the roots, assuming that any creativity after the Bible was only an exegesis of the Bible. The root is considered with the origin and the original.

Though we are emphasizing creativity in the sense of ideas and their literary manifestations, the coming back to the land of Israel also had the very significant connotation of establishing a society, an in-gathering of people. In this sense, Zionism absorbed the major trends of the national movements of Europe, giving them a particular meaning because of the Jewish situation. It is not only an emancipation from a political yoke, but also a return in the more literal sense of that word.

Renaissance amounts to the reestablishment of Jewish cohesion and independence, which had been lost in the situation.

⁂ ⁂ ⁂

Within the contemporary cultural situation of the state of Israel, we can discern some significant aspects related to the notion of renaissance. There is, for instance, a great interest in Israel in archaeological relics, exemplifying renaissance as a return to the real vestiges of the past, that is to say, to those survivals that represent the reality of the past and are objects of interest in the present. Looking for the past, we find it physically represented in its relics. There is no identity between the return to the roots of creativity and interest in the survivals, but there is apparently some parallelism between the two.

We should be aware of the problem of duality in the effort to be free of the impact of the past on the one hand, and in the return to the root of roots, the Bible, on the other. Also in this context, it becomes obvious that a historical reality is not determined by one component only, for it is essentially a conglomerate of components. In this particular context we have the conjunction of coming back to the origin of life and of coming back to the origin of creativity. To be sure, within the development of Zionist ideology we find attempts to establish a synthesis of a more harmonious character between these components. Thus, for instance, Ahad Ha'am emphasizes the notion of coming back to the roots of creativity and not that of the infrastructure of reality, whereas, Aharon David Gordon[3] represents the attempt to establish a connection between these two components; return to life is by the same token a return to the roots both in the sense of ideas and in the sense of the Jewish religion, based on man's relation to the cosmos.

※ ※ ※

There is also a third component within the connotation of renaissance that cannot be seen as determined within and by the Jewish internal context. The first two components, because of their connection of concrete historical reality, are concerned with the new momentum to be given to the creative capacity of the Jewish people. The third, very common in everyday vocabulary, is what is called normalization. Normalization is a creating of a structure of other people, but also as adhering to a norm, and this norm is conceived as a conjunction of the three factors—territorial basis, society, and the authority of the state. Normal people are those who in their day-to-day reality live within a structure composed of these three factors.

If we think of ideologists who can be considered as representing this particular direction of thought, we turn to those who conceived political Zionism—J. L. Pinsker and Theodore Herzl. Concern with normalcy also led to the analysis of Jewish society, including the economic system characteristic of Jews in the Diaspora. Jews were considered as non-normal because their existence was based on activities that were not related to the primary aspects of economic life, like agriculture and industry.

From this point of view, normalization led to the demand to change the character of Jewish society and encourage people to work in agriculture and industry. This direction can be considered as an extension of the concept of normalization, in the sense of not being confined only to the structural aspects of Jewish reality but also to its infrastructure. In any event, the different interpretations of renaissance expressed and influenced different ideological concerns. Since we have emphasized the cohesion of the different interpretations and mentioned some typological examples, we should now inquire into the contemporary interpretation of renaissance and also whether it in fact exists.

※ ※ ※

To analyze the contemporary situation in light of the concept of renaissance it might be useful to make some additional comments on the revitalization aspect. This may shed some light on the impact of the other components of the concept of renaissance.

If we understand revitalization to the broad sense as giving a new momentum to Jewish activity, grounded in the dynamics of the present Jewish existence, we can say that in the last eighty or a hundred years we encounter an accelerated process of these dynamics. It would be one-sided to argue that only a certain conception had an impact on this process, since Jewish existence is, of course, connected to the broad context of historical reality. The emigration of Jews from their countries of origin, mainly to the United States, is significant in this context. Furthermore, a change occurred in the modes of Jewish behavior and the destruction of European Jewry can be placed in this context. It changed the profile of the Jewish people, transferring its center and attention from a folk character to that of the centers of modern civilization. One cannot say, however, that all these aspects belong to revitalization in the programmatic sense of that term. As far as coming back to the roots of Jewish existence and bringing "new blood" to that existence are concerned, when we look at the actual process, we can say that the various components brought different factors into the texture of reality. From the point of view of characterizing the process, we are justified in saying that the dynamics of Jewish history over the last hundred years is an accelerated one. This characteristic feature is not unrelated to the general trends of history, accelerated movements being characteristic of recent generations and of culture in general.

If we now look again at this meaning of return—to the roots or revitalizing those roots—we observe that the trend toward return is quite common in various national movements and aspirations. The reestablishment of national independence is a focal point in these tendencies, because in many cases there is an attempt to reestablish the independence of people who have lost it and aspire to reacquire it. Thus the component of reestablishment, that is, not creating a reality from the very beginning, is an attractive factor in various national movements. The unification of Italy had an impact, for instance, as mentioned above, on the thought of Moses Hess. He took it as the prime example of returning to the aspired reality of a people and as a paradigm for a solution of the Jewish national problem, which he considered the last of the national problems. We may add something intrinsic to Jewish culture, namely, the fact that it is a culture related to the past and to its origin in the Bible, while Jewish creativity, both in the domain of ideas and in the literary sense, considered itself an exegesis of the Scriptures. Thus we can understand that the notion of a return to roots was grounded in Jewish thought or self-awareness throughout the ages and in the particular components of the Jewish people within the historical process. The notion of tradition, which is so prominent, is obviously a manifestation of that aspect.

To be sure, the notion of return in this sense was formulated in a historical reality differing from our contemporary environment. It was formulated in the context of Eastern and Central European Jewry and in connection with the emergence of modern Hebrew literature and Jewish thought. It would be sentimental or idyllic to consider the centers of Jewish creativity in Odessa and Warsaw and to see the shift to Jerusalem as nonproblematic. Yet if we take the notion of revitalization and renaissance in its basic sense, we can say that even when the context of reality changes, the tension and the possible connection between that notion and the problematic character of historical reality is retained. The notion of revitalization must come to grips with accelerated historical processes, that is to say, in the contemporary context, with the great changes in the demographic infrastructure of the Jewish people, with the encounter with new populations and their cultural modes. Broadly speaking, continuity, both factual and that of consciousness, is not as strong as in previous generations. We may say that Eastern European Jewry, in relation to which the conception of renaissance was formulated and debated, presupposed explicitly or not, the existence of historical continuity and historical consciousness. Rejuvenation was to occur against the background of that continuity. Regarding the situation in the contemporary era, we cannot say that the continuity of consciousness can be taken for granted. We have to reconstruct that continuity against the background of the new modes of existence. This applies both to the Diaspora and to Israeli society, with all the differences between these two basic structures of the Jewish people in the present era.

Because of this new situation—the renaissance must both maintain historical consciousness of continuity and re-establish it—we face the problem of the meaning of the return to the roots of Jewish creativity. We are citizens of the world and at the same time we attempt to maintain not only the territorial definition of the Jews but also their historical continuity. We face a universal culture, which is no longer basically a culture grounded in historical religions, mainly Christianity. With all the impact of Christianity on the world, it could always be conceived as a partial culture and as such grounded, at least to some extent, however antithetically, in Judaism. In present-day reality, we face a culture that does not consider itself derived from religious sources. It is a culture that presents itself as one of man as such without any addendum. It is based on free-thinking, directed to an analysis of the world and understanding it. It is a scientific culture and its product, which, to some extent, even overshadows its basis, namely the technological civilization, is based on methodology and not on content. Its influence is in the direction of emphasizing the welfare of human beings and thus guiding them toward the future, making the historical sources, at least to some extent, obsolete. Jews not only absorb these trends, but actively emphasize them and enhance their impact. Thus we no longer live in a situation in which one historical culture faces another one or even clashes with it. We live in an open civilization that not only absorbs remnants of the past but lets them belong to the past without assuming that they should shape the future.

To be sure, within the Jewish reality of the state of Israel an infrastructure of continuity exists, expressed in the continuous presence of the Hebrew language. That presence is not only of a communicative significance, but also directs attention to the roots of the language in the Scriptures. Indeed, the Bible holds a basic position within the Israeli school curricula. In addition, there are segments of society that do not accept the duality of universality and adherence to the established modes of Jewish behavior. For them, what is universal is universal mainly of an instrumental validity, and without an impact on the orientation of society and the individual.

※ ※ ※

When we look at the aspect of normalization, we again encounter a very particular situation. Broadly speaking we are a non-normal people, within which there is a process toward normalization. In fact, we live in a framework that can be looked at as a norm and as normalcy. There is a Jewish territorial basis and a Jewish society manifesting itself within the state of Israel, and there is also a Jewish sovereignty. Still, we live in a mode of reality that cannot be considered normal for two significant reasons. On the one hand, we are in the process of establishing a state that is both the state of the society living in it and of the whole Jewish people, the majority of whom do not live in it. Somehow we have difficulty in formulating this situation and we may wonder whether there are accepted conceptual tools for that formulation. The society within the state can be socially or sociologically characterized, whereas the Jewish people for whom the state of Israel is its state, does not present an established way of expressing its position in accepted sociological terms. There is a duality between concrete existence in the present and the historical entity still manifested in the Jewish people, vague as that concept may be. There is an additional particular aspect to the situation, because normalization being the acceptance of the common norms of ethnic reality, has brought about conflicts within the Jewish framework, even within the society of the state of Israel, expressed mainly in the impact of the traditional mode of religion on day-to-day existence and its orientations. The presence of the Arab population within the state of Israel makes the duality between the society inside the state and of it and the Jewish people even more visible.

We can sum up by saying that the notion of normalization was formulated in an international political reality different from that dominant in the present era. As the conception of renaissance was formulated in a different reality, so the conception of normalization was formulated in a liberal mode of existence and it was assumed that if one determines one's own identity, that determination will be accepted by one's fellows, not only on the individual level but also that of groups, societies, and states. Let us recall the saying of an Austrian poet that the hard core of the liberal idea is to live and let live. Because of the changes that have occurred in historical trends, the principle of normality is for us the entrance into the real history of the world. That history is not characterized by conflicts alone, but our entrance into it has sharpened the conflict, mainly between ourselves and Arab nationalism.

In any case, we face a new problematic situation and within it we are aware or should be aware that any solution creates a new problem and in this sense, gives rise to a dialectical process, which imposes on us a new formulation of the old problem. This might be considered a characteristic feature of historical reality in general. It is not, as was thought in the eighteenth century, a process that in a linear way leads to a desired goal and thus creates progress, which amounts also to a nonproblematic situation. Since we are trying to maintain the various components of renaissance and normalcy, we must be aware of that problematic situation. Paradoxically we have to adhere to the components without assuming their harmonious materialization. This situation has a central additional focus related to the impact of tradition mainly on renaissance within Israeli society.

As we have seen, renaissance amounts to coming back. That very notion implies a sort of skipping over that which is present in order to return to some basic position of the past, which is both classical as a paradigm and normative as that which has to be followed. The normative aspect is inherent in tradition, in the Jewish context. Because tradition relates to the Bible and to the Talmudic literature, assuming that there is continuity from the Scriptures to Talmudic creativity, both present concepts and imperatives of day-to-day behavior. Continuity as such is understood as a norm or even as the norm of Jewish existence in spite of the changes, which are inherent in the historical process and which have their impact on the day-to-day behavior of the Jews, let alone the existence of the Jewish state.

Tradition is therefore a mode of continuous existence both factually and normatively, whereby the reception of that which comes from the past is the fundamental aspect of tradition. Tradition is transmission and not innovation or to put it differently, the historical process is the preservation of canons of behavior. Zionism, attempting to arrive at the renaissance of Jewish creativity, faces the question whether renaissance can be congruous with accepting the transmission or if it contains the components of innovation though that innovation may be the other side of the coin of coming back to some basis of Jewish existence as the return to the land of Israel implies. Concurrently, Zionism aimed at the establishment of the Jewish collective existence inherent in the public realm. It is obvious that the tradition to which Diaspora Jews refer in their day-to-day existence, they refer to as individuals, but not to the public realm because that realm just did not exist. The establishment of the realm is already an innovation and thus amounts to the inevitable fact that tradition has to face that innovation. Hence we find both an innovation in terms of a new mode of existence, which is by definition of central relevance, and what can be called the selection of traditional facets, which are inherent in the notion of return. It has to be mentioned in this context that without the connection with Zionism, nineteenth-century Jewry already defined that which can be called the selective interpretations of tradition as opposed to the accumulative interpretations of it, which was the major point of view of the previous generations. The selective position by definition deals with tradition as the background, and not as a totality, which has to be accepted as such. Because of different considerations, Zionism takes the attitude of selection inspired by the basic position of collective existence as against the continuity as it has been shaped all over the generations. Negatively speaking, Halakha could not be taken as absolute as it appears in some contemporary discussions or as is assumed to be normative for Halakha that Jewish law does not change because of the new situation. No situation is entitled to give rise to a change.

It is appropriate to mention here the writings of the great Talmudic scholar Professor Ephraim Urbach, who precisely because he adhered to Halakha, tried to reformulate the aspect of faith inherent in it as well as the position of the human mind, which cannot be pushed aside because it is called to transmit the heritage of the previous generations to the present-day position. Indeed, Urbach emphasized the component of present-day reality to which tradition has to apply and, which, at least at the beginning, has to be taken as one of the poles of reality that cannot be pushed aside against the background of return on the one hand and construction of a new reality on the other.[4]

Renaissance has also been understood and—this is rather common in many circles of Israeli society—as the awareness of continuity and not as acceptance of the norms formulated in the Halakhic literature with all the interpretations that went along with it. We can add an additional comment that precisely because the society of Israel is meant to be comprehensive society, it has to integrate, if at all, the ritualistic aspect of Halakah into the context of the broad scope of reality. From this point of view, the situation of Israeli society and the inherent trends of its existence differ from the Jewish situation in the Diaspora where because there is no comprehensive mode of existence, the peripheral aspect of rituals can be understood as predominant, moreover because they are meant to be the preserving factors of Jewish existence or the affiliation of the Jews to their continuous historical mode of existence.

We could say that there exists a traditional interpretation of tradition, if we may use this self-reflective or paradoxical conjunction. According to that interpretation, there is no significance of the Jewish people as a collective and as individuals. The people are under a fundamental obligation to accept the norms of tradition. The problem this interpretation faced, related to the self-awareness of the Jews who tried to live in their contemporary reality and in the environmental world, without accepting a priori the guidance of the norms inherent in tradition. There emerged from this point of view a basic change in the Jewish situation in the contemporary era mainly within the state of Israel. The reality is not imposed by outside factors. It has been the goal of the Jews and "the realization in reality" poses problems, which could not be present in the previous generations because of the comprehensive character of that new reality. In terms of that character, there is no distinction between that which belongs to the Jewish reality and that which is a part of the environment. Everything is by definition within the one comprehensive reality. Economic problems are part of Jewish reality as language and the adherence to the past are. There is no distinction within the comprehensive reality between being a human being and a Jew.

For Diaspora Jewry, the problem is precisely because Jews are involved in the comprehensive reality that is not their own, neither historically nor as the goal of their existence. The question is how to preserve tradition vis-à-vis this peripheral mode of existence. The problem Israeli society is facing is how to preserve tradition within the spectrum of their reality as it is. We can point to a very significant manifestation of that problem, namely the legislation of the state is grounded in the vote of the people and their representatives. They may be inspired by tradition, but the act as such is a manifestation of the democratic structure of the society and the state, and is not a continuation of the norms of tradition.

These can be incorporated in the contents of legislation, but they cannot replace the legislation as such being an act and not a content. Even when the legislation accords a special position to the rabbinic courts and therefore by definition to the norms guiding their decisions, the status of the rabbinic court is grounded in the decision of the legislative body of the state of Israel, and it is not accepted as being inherited from the traditional structure of Jewish existence. This problem is inherent in Israeli society and its direction. From this point of view, there is a paradoxical difference between Jewry in the Diaspora and the Jewish character of Israeli society. Jewry in the Diaspora has to struggle with the problem of tradition, because its daily existence is not shaped by the adherence to Jewish norms but by their own comprehensive society. Israeli society faces a problem of tradition, because of its comprehensive character and because whatever has to be relevant to be valid, has to be incorporated in the structure of the society. There are indeed Jews who do not accept the structure of Israeli society and of the state of Israel as such, but as long as they live in that society, they cannot escape the necessity or even the compulsion to come to grips at least factually with that character.

At this point, we can say that the renaissance is not only a return, but an innovation.

Notes

1. Renaissance does not have the limited meaning of "restoration of letters." It is applied to broad situation which tries to continue the adherence to the past prominent channels of activity in the present directed to shaping the future. See Huizinga's analysis referred to before.

2. Berdichevsky Micha Joseph (also spelled Berdyczweski), a writer and publicist. (His Hebrew name is Bin Gorion). In his Hebrew and Yiddish articles he advocated the "transvaluation" of the Jewish accepted modes of behavior.

3. Gordon, Aharon David grounds his analysis of the situation of the Jewish in a philosophical conception. According to it, a people is a unit in the realm of nature and even of the cosmos. A people is destined to be a "people-man" (am-adam). Labor, lacking in the Jewish situation as it is will be a return to nature. A selection of his writings in an English Translation: Selected Essays, is available.

4. Urbach, Ephraim Elimelech, On Zionism and Judaism (in Hebrew), 1985.

Chapter 4

The Negation of the Diaspora

The "negation of the Diaspora" has an evaluative, not a factual meaning, that is, it is not the existence of the Diaspora that is negated (in some ideological trends), but the position of the Diaspora as the Jewish mode of life. That negative evaluation is meant to serve as a stimulus toward an ideological formulation circumscribing Jewish reality. By the same token it is an incentive toward overcoming that reality and establishing a new and different mode of Jewish existence in the Land of Israel, or in the contemporary context, the state of Israel.

Zionism reinforced the attitude of evaluative negation, an attitude inherent in the very notion of Diaspora. Diaspora is a common translation of Galut or Golah, epitomizing the dispersion of the Jewish people. Another (or complementary) term commonly used in Western language to denote this condition is "exile," derived from Latin and originally connoting banishment and penalty, stressing rather the constraint that forces people to live outside their native or original land. We could say that expatriation is the common core both of Diaspora and of exile, since dispersion is the outcome of the removal of a group or people from their original territorial base. The negative evaluation contained in the concept and in the terms meant to designate it is reinforced by a combination of two aspects of constraint, both in terms of origin (as exile) and of results (as dispersion).

This negative evaluation of the Golah is inherent in the historical consciousness of the Jewish people and its tradition. It was further reinforced by the attempt to place the Golah in a broader context, for instance the view that the reality of the Golah is the consequence of sin—because of our sins we were expelled from our land. Inasmuch as the exile and the Diaspora were understood as punishment, this interpretation reinforced the negative evaluation of the situation. Hence both the reality and its cause were exposed to negation—in the evaluative sense.

This does not mean that the situation was totally repudiated, since, for instance, one of the notions current in historical consciousness was that the divine reality is manifested in the presence of the Jews in the Diaspora, as expressed in the traditional concept that the divine presence itself is in the Golah. That correlation between the position of the people and the position of the divine entity was meant to be—at least to some extent—a kind of consolation formulated in the context of the special relation of the people and God.

※ ※ ※

The negative attitude toward the Golah is in the background to the Zionist conception in its classical reformulation in the modern age. Since it is a major modern trend to consider historical reality as detached from extra- or supra-historical causes (as analyzed before) classical Zionist ideology continued to evaluate the Diaspora negatively without relating that evaluation to the notion of sin. The basic approach of Zionist ideology has been to explore reality as such, recognizing its various characteristic components and trends. That recognition led to the formulation of the negative aspect of the situation. One might say that since modernity in general is characterized by an understanding of the immanent position of nature as well as that of history, the modern analysis of the character of the Diaspora brings that approach to the fore.

An attempt was thus made to see the historical position of the Diaspora in terms of its built-in components, leading to the denial of the possibility of maintaining national Jewish existence within a Diaspora context. Not only were the very dispersion and compulsion negatively evaluated but also the everyday existence. As a result, the rejection of the possibility of resolving the inherent problems of Jewish existence within the framework of existing reality became forceful.

Furthermore, in the traditional interpretations of the Diaspora, its negative aspects are due to be resolved at the messianic end of time. Zionism is based on the assumption that not only should the historical reality be examined in its internal aspects, but the solution to its problems is to be sought in intervention by living human beings in the current historical era.

Hence the presupposition is that the solution to the problem or problems of the Diaspora can be found only in the historical acts of the Jews as human beings dwelling in reality and called on to share it. In the traditional approach to the Diaspora we encounter a sort of reciprocity between the supra-historical position and the supra-historical resolution of that position, whereas in modern Zionist ideology we encounter a reciprocity between the historical position of the Diaspora and historical intervention directed toward solving those essential difficulties that can be brought under the heading of the Diaspora problem as such.

In this context we encounter the notion of what has been described as the ex-territorial existence of the Jewish people. The very essence of the Diaspora is understood as being ex-territorial and that notion or term contains its own negative evaluation. This negative evaluation is by the same token a rejection, inviting attempts to overcome it and continuously promoting them.

At this point an additional component of ex-territorial existence emerges. That existence is the fundamental cause for modes of living that are to be rejected both from the point of view of the national collectivity as well as from that of its social and normal aspects, related in the first place to the economic activities of the Jewish people in the Diaspora. Historically speaking, the Socialist trend in Zionsim paid major attention to the economic, social, and moral aspects of Jewish reality, prompting the conclusion that there was no solution within the boundaries of the Diaspora itself to the problems inherent in the modes of living of the Jewish people. That conclusion is meant to demonstrate that, since the very ex-territorial basis of Jewish existence is to be negatively evaluated, nothing positive can develop against such a background. It should be stressed that the analysis of the economic modes of existence—an analysis inherent in Socialist Zionism—reflects the mood of modernity, that is to say the identification of the day-to-day modes of human reality and their impact on the Jewish position. Aharon David Gordon characterized the occupations of the Jews in the Diaspora as "parasitic."

The great historian Yitzhak Baer has shown in his study of the Galut,[1] that at the very beginning of the modern age, the economic activities of the Jews gave rise to negative reflections, for instance in Jewish thought in seventeenth-century Italy. Attempts were made to show that the characterization of the Jews as financial middlemen or moneylenders in the Middle Ages was related not to their predilections or nature but to their imposed position on the fringes of non-Jewish society. Broadly speaking, their occupations were the result of the Diaspora as such. What was negatively evaluated even in traditional thought by way of scattered reflection has become a central issue in some trends of Zionist ideology.[2]

※ ※ ※

We may begin with the position formulated by Ahad Ha'am to which we have already alluded. Ahad Ha'am was one of the first Zionist thinkers to popularize the term "negation of the Diaspora." In his view, the major unfavorable aspect of the Diaspora consisted in what he described as the contraction of the national "ego." That ego added up to the sum total of creativity of a people, being also the propelling and inspiring factor in that creativity. The existence of the Jewish people in the Diaspora is necessarily constrained by the contraction of its creativity because of exposure to the outside world and the limitation of its basic activities to only some avenues of that creativity. The culture of the surrounding society penetrates into Jewish existence to such an extent that contraction is a necessary product of this continuous exposure to the outside world. The concept of the spiritual center, the focus of Ahad Ha'am's ideology, arises from that unavoidable Diaspora situation. The establishment of a center for Jewish creativity would be a focus of the renaissance of the national ego of the Jewish people, having a status of its own within its own boundaries, alongside the status of the Diaspora factors, in order to neutralize the negated impact of the outside world.

To look at this from a different angle, we might say that Ahad Ha'am's conclusion was that the Diaspora itself, out of its own resources, was unable to solve its inherent problem. This should be stressed, though Ahad Ha'am himself, as is well known, did not assume the possibility of resolving, that is, overcoming the ex-territorial position of the Jewish people. This was the main difference between his and Herzl's ideological positions. As compared to a radical solution to ex-territoriality, Ahad Ha'am suggested a solution that can be seen as a prudent or then more realistic one, related to the influence of the spiritual center to be established in the Land of Israel. The reference is to the overall creativity of the people, which cannot be carried on within Diaspora boundaries. This situation would prevail even if the impact of the cultural center were to be palpable.

One of the consequences of that view was that analysis of the Diaspora situation led to the conclusion that although the Diaspora cannot itself revive its creativity, adjustment to the de facto situation is necessary and unavoidable. To put it differently, the Diaspora is negated in terms of possible creativity but affirmed as a fact in terms of the unlikely eventuality that it will be resolved by a total retreat from the Diaspora situation.

Against that background, Ahad Ha'am put forward a distinction that is central to his view, on the one hand, and to the understanding of the broad concept of the negation of the Diaspora, on the other. He says that the negation of the Diaspora amounts necessarily to the objective negation, that is to say, to a position that denies the possibility of maintaining the national existence of the Jewish people in the generations to come. Once the spiritual home has been diminished, as the home that was our forefather's shelter in past generations, there is no escape from the impact of the surrounding external cultures. That culture now absorbs all the national assets of the Jews, and step by step may bring about an end to their existence as a people.

That analysis of the Diaspora is the "objective" attitude. The very fact that the Diaspora has the shape it has, elicits objective negation. In spite of that analysis and its consequences we must distinguish between the fact that the Diaspora exists, with all its inherent shortcomings and dangers, and what Ahad Ha'am calls its subjective negation. We negate the Diaspora in our consciousness in spite of the fact that there is no way but to affirm its de facto objective existence. Perhaps we would not now use the phrase "objective affirmation" but "adjustment" or "acceptance." But the terminological nuance does not alter the distinction suggested by Ahad Ha'am between the objective or factual situation on the one hand and our attitude to it in terms of the inevitable future on the other.

A historical comment may be made at this juncture: The context in which Ahad Ha'am formulated his view was that of the proposed autonomy of the Jewish people or the Jewish population in the Diaspora—a view propagated by Shimon Dubnow.[3] Ahad Ha'am rejected that proposal because it had no likelihood of success and because of its propagating an inherent illusion related to the possible mitigation of the objective situation through the autonomy of the Jewish population within Diaspora boundaries.

※ ※ ※

We move now to a different interpretation of the Diaspora in terms of its negative features or, perhaps more strongly, in terms of its very situation: the views of Brenner[4] and Berdichevsky.[5]

It may be no accident that these two were novelists as well as ideologues. They apply their negative evaluation of the Diaspora to the day-to-day character of Jewish existence and not only to the contraction inherent in it. Brenner even uses a traditional term, a loaded one, saying that there is sinfulness in Diaspora existence itself; the focus of the sin is the fact that people cease to work. This broad statement, seemingly a description, can be understood as referring not only to the economic and social aspects of the basis of Jewish existence in the Diaspora. What is significant is the consequence of the socioeconomic infrastructure and its impact on the psychic and spiritual aspects of that existence. Hence the Diaspora situation is not only an economic deformation but also a kind of human stigma.

A variation on the same theme can be seen in Berdichevsky's view that the sin committed by the Jewish people was their too great haste to leave their own country, giving priority to the commercial aspects of human reality.

This formulation obviously implies the argument that the existence of the Diaspora is not only a result of compulsion. It is a result of what the Jewish people decided as its move of daily existence. That view led to the conclusion that the ghetto lacked the potential for any existence imbued with creativity. There is a component of redemption in the very creativity of a people; hence the traditional distinction between redemption and the Diaspora is transferred to the antithesis between the basis of the Diaspora and its possible creativity. To put this differently, we may say that we encounter here an analysis that does not point only to the social and economic aspects of the Diaspora but also, and mainly, to its human aspects as epitomized in cultural creativity. Berdichevsky formulates that position very bluntly: Judaism contains ideas but Jews live in the mud.

In summing up, we come to the following conclusions. Ahad Ha'am negated the Diaspora because of its inherent essence, but he adjusted himself to it and tried to find a prudent solution to its problems outside its own context. Brenner and Berdichevsky sharpened the negative attitude by pronouncing extreme views—because of the far-reaching deficiencies of its existence there is no solution to the Diaspora problem except by total denial and hence exodus. There is no way for coexistence between the Diaspora and that which is outside it, since there is no way for a partial therapy for the inherent malady of the Diaspora condition.

In his *Exile and Alienation* Yehezkel Kaufman[6] does not accept the descriptive—or what can be called the empirical—characterization of the Jewish mode of existence in the Diaspora. He views the ghetto not as a moral evil but as a national disaster. Any argument against this tendency, such as referring to Jewish creativity in the Diaspora, is not accepted. The Diaspora must be seen as an alien environment, as the title of his book indicates. The very environment of the Diaspora calls for its rejection. One may assume that the practical conclusion to be drawn from that situation according to Kaufman would be to get out of it. As the emphasis is put on the environment of the Diaspora as such, Kaufman does not analyze its impact on the day-to-day existence Jews are exposed to. Awareness of alienation is considered to be the core of the situation on one hand and a motivating factor on the other. Unlike a pragmatic analysis of the various trends mentioned before, Kaufman's position can be described as a nominal presentation of the state of affairs of the Diaspora as such, and a call for awareness of the strangeness inherent in exile.

To put it differently, Jews will not be able to maintain their global identity without a focus, placed not within the context of their scattered existence but outside it. That focus is not identical with a substance or a context but is the symbol of what can be described as a sentimental belonging or affiliation. The State of Israel serves that purpose, it has become a center for Jewish content. This process of looking for a focus is the other side of the openness of the environment toward the Jews and of the Jews toward it. We encounter here a kind of reversal of the motto of the Jewish Enlightenment—one should be a Jew at home and a human being outside it. It turns out that within one's own home there is almost no distinction between the Jewish mode of living and that of other people. Therefore Jews tend to manifest their belonging to a framework of Jewish existence by exhibiting it in organizational terms of emphasizing the framework without the substance. This process is related to the mode of living and that of other people. Therefore Jews tend to manifest their belonging to a framework of Jewish existence by exhibiting it in organizational terms of emphasizing the framework without the substance. This process is related to the trend of modern culture, which has ceased to be historical, let alone religious. This decisive significance of science and technology leads toward a universal culture both on the highest level of creativity as well as on that of popular expression. It was easier, apparently, to maintain a Jewish historical culture, including the religious substance, within an environment imbued with historical trends than to maintain a historical culture within an environment characterized by the trend toward a universal culture. In that situation the State of Israel serves as a sentimental focus of the present.

Jews who leave the sphere of traditional Judaism do not undergo soul-searching or conscientious misgivings—probably because they are not leaving behind a historical culture of their own for the sake of another historical culture: they are joining mankind. The Diaspora negates itself by enhancing the awareness that it is no longer exile. Hence an evaluation of the Diaspora position in terms of the modes of Jewish existence loses its ground. What was negation from the point of view of the Jewish position has become disappearance from the point of view of the processes to which the collective Jewish entity is exposed. The locus of these processes is the Diaspora in the Western world. With the disappearance of the aspect of alienation from the Jewish horizon we find a progressive disappearance of the collective existence of the Jews. The presentness of the State of Israel is not a motivating factor toward the withdrawal from the Diaspora. The State of Israel fails to be a spiritual center, not because of its shortcomings, but because of the disparity between a historical center and the universal trends of modernity. The state reinforces the static aspects of Jewish existence or in a stronger term, the inertia of the Jews: it is not a dynamic factor pointing to a different mode of Jewish loyalty and the environment. Classical Zionist ideology did not envisage these processes: and probably could not, since prediction in history is more than problematic.

※ ※ ※

The characteristic feature of the various trends, which, in a sense, were a conjunction of social orientations and ideological or normative presentations, was an attitude of self-analysis and self-criticism. Those who criticized day-to-day Diaspora of the previous centuries, criticized themselves. That quality added more than a touch of authenticity to their criticism; also, some of the critics were writers of imaginative literature that gave their thinking an authentic, emotional expression.

In comparison, Western Jewry to a very large extent lacks this attitude of self-awareness and self-criticism and one may assume that without the disposition toward self-analysis and openness to self-criticism there is little chance for the formulation of a serious, profound, ideological analysis.[7]

Modernity has profound bearings on the contemporary ideological situation of Jewry. Self-satisfaction does not go well with self-criticism. Underlying the modern or postmodern trend is the conviction, explicit or otherwise, that those problems that have not yet been solved will find a solution in the course of the process itself. This kind of optimism is again an inhibiting factor in formulating an ideology that is both analytic and perspective, and call for intervention in the process.

To be sure, the differences in the essence of the situation cannot be overlooked. Even granted that anti-Jewish or anti-Semitic trends and manifestations were bound to be present in societies Jews lived in, reality in Eastern Europe was overwhelming. Moreover, when anti-Semitic manifestations were common in societies, the state authorities were expected to act against them and restrict anti-Semitic expressions and persecution, defamation, and denial of the rights of Jews to take part in day-to-day activities. Nevertheless, Western Diaspora has brought into prominence a basic aspect of Jewish reality in modern or postmodern times, that is, the lack of continuity between the life of the individual Jew and that of the Jewish Society or commonwealth.

As long as Jews were characterized by modes of everyday behavior, the belonging to the Jewish people was inherent and reinforced in their individual existence. The contemporary situation is characterized by the lack of that continuity and mutual reinforcement. Hence belonging to the Jewish commonwealth is more an aspiration or a sentiment than a day-to-day mode of behavior. It goes much further than what was envisaged in the classical formulations as the contraction of the Jewish national self since the surrounding world is not open to that kind of continuity between individuals and the collectivity, because of the anti-historical, or at least the a-historical, direction of the world: the historical past is no longer of significance for everyday reality.

We can almost guess the direction, or the ideology, of Jewish education in the modern world. The emphasis, explicit or not, is on the survival of the Jewish people, and not on the continuation of its creativity. Education contracted to the goal of survival is obviously directed to a minimal goal. We may wonder whether it can be at all fruitful if this education is not directed to the potentiality of the learner, but to this learner's position as an element in the continuity of existence of the Jewish people. Continuity is certainly significant, but when creativity is taken as a goal, survival as such would be a by-product of the enhancement of the individual potential creativity.

There is probably a relation between the growing number of intermarriages in the Western Diaspora and the minimal goal of Jewish education, and even more so when many Jewish children attend general schools.[8]

These comments on aspects of the modern Jewish situation are not intended to ignore or set aside the fundamental changes occurring in Jewish reality. Hence it is impossible and inappropriate to apply to modern Western society, and to the Jews living in it, the formulations and findings of the classic Zionist ideology. We must face the situation as it is, and disclose the problematic aspects in this ideology, which are not an outcome of misjudgment or misunderstanding the situation, but the other side of the openness of modern society. This clash between modern society and the continuity of the Jewish people within it is at the same time the frontage of that openness, and the price modern Jewish existence must pay.

※ ※ ※

We are bound to come to the conclusion that emancipation cannot replace auto-emancipation, though the latter is a sort of continuation of the former. To put it in context of the differences between survival and creativity we could say that without creativity there is no survival. Creativity can be maintained only within the framework of auto-emancipation, that is, within the limits of a plausible continuity between the life of individuals and the life of the collectivity.

This is not to say that the continuity is harmonious or that the modes of existence of the Jewish people in the State of Israel are not inherently imbued with many problems. We noticed that aspect in speaking of tradition against the background of renaissance. But the problematic situation of the State of Israel is of a different order from that of modern Western Jewry.

This should be the main point of departure for a new formulation of the Zionist ideology. The core of that formulation would be the awareness that the negation of the Diaspora cannot be focused on the repudiation of aspects of the perverted Jewish reality in the Diaspora. Rather it should focus on the locality of that Diaspora, as it is impossible to maintain Jewish collectivity within the given framework of existence in the Dispora.

There is indeed an interaction between awareness in the ideological sense and decision in the existential sense. One may wonder where to take the first step: to analyze the situation calls for a decision, and the analysis may bring about a voluntary action. In that sense, even more than in previous generations, awareness of the Diaspora and the outcome in the direction would most probably be confined to the elite of the Jewish people. It would be an elite of a different character, not in terms of profession or intellectual standing but in terms of conviction and the commitment nourished by it. The Diaspora negates itself—actually and obviously—but not prescriptively. Where does Jewry go from here?

In the previous chapters we have already outlined aspects of Zionist ideology related to the Jewish situation as it is now. It is our task to move toward a systematic explication of these aspects. Jews are not reminded of their origins. The conservation based on opposition ceases to be part of the "climate of opinion of the Jews." There is no conservation except that based on inner Jewish factors and motivation. The reformulation of the Zionist ideology becomes mandatory not only for preserving the continuity of ideology but mainly for the sake of the question of existence.

Notes

1. Yitzhak F. Baer: *Galut*, 1988.

2. The interrelation between the religious orientation of society at large and the religious adherence of the Jews to their religion

was stressed by Immanuel Kant: "{the Jews} have continued to maintain themselves as such, though scattered throughout the world; whereas the faith of other religious fellowships has usually been fused with the faith of the people among whom they have been scattered." . . ."What the Jews would not have achieved of themselves, the Christian and later the Mohammedan religions brought about—especially the former: for these religions presupposed the Jewish faith and the sacred books belonging to it." . . . "Hence we find no Jews outside the countries referred to." . . . "Although it cannot be doubted that they spread throughout those rich lands, yet because of the lack of all kinship between their faith and the types of belief found there, they came wholly to forget their own." Immanuel Kant: *Religion within the Limits of Reason Alone*, trans. And with an introduction and notes by Theodore M. Greene and Hoyt H. Hudson, p. 12 (note). One could describe the contemporary situation as one not basically akin to the Jewish adherence to sacred books. Jews do not have an external incentive to maintain their own faith.

3. Shimon Dubnow, author of the ten volumes: *History of the Jewish people*, believed that the future survival of the Jews as a nation depended on their spiritual and cultural strength, and self-rule in the Diaspora. This ideology is known as Jewish Autonomism.

4. Brenner, Joseph Chaim, a Hebrew writer and idealogue.

5. Berdichevsky is discussed also in chapter 3 above.

6. The book *Golah Venechar* (Golah and Strangeness), published in Tel Aviv 1929–1932 is available in Hebrew only. The subtitle reads: a historical–sociological study of the question of the fate of the people of Israel from ancient times to the present day.

7. Ben Halperin's *The American Jew: A Zionist Analysis* (N.Y. 1956) is an analysis grounded in Zionism—possibly the only one of this sort.

8. Expressions of that self-examination are rather scarce. Attention should be given to Stuart E. Eizenstadt's comment: "The path we choose will not be dictated, as has been the case for virtually all of Jewish history, by our external enemies. It will be determined by us. Our challenge is not the external foe of anti-Semitism, but the self-administered poison of excessive assimilation." (JCC Circle. June, 1990). To be sure, the direction of the activity proposed in this paper, cannot overcome the peripheral character of Jewish existence in an open society.

Chapter 5

The Values of Israeli Society

We have considered several aspects of Zionism, both the historical trends and the ideological commitment. The establishment of Israel is a realization of Zionism in its various components. Reality as realization has an impact on the underlying ideology. That impact must be considered also from the perspective of the values of Israeli society. Values belong more to the ideological horizons of a society than to its empirical situation, whereas the *morals* of a society, sometimes snapped by traumatic experiences like wars, has a bearing on its ideologically guiding principles. The term *morals* connotes by and large the position of an individual or a group of individuals characterized by stability, self-confidence, a positive expectation of the future, as well as the readiness to make decisions and to act in order to promote goals, which will be realized in the future. In this sense morale, both individual and social, is grounded in sets of values. Values are principles that guide action and self-awareness as well as the choice of goals toward which effort will be directed.

This analysis will look into some basic human and cultural problems of Israeli society. These are basic questions, since they do not emerge from a specific dramatic or traumatic situation, though such situations may make the problems more concrete or more acute. They are basic since they related to the texture of Israeli society and its aspirations as well as to its historical and cultural background. The articulation of these issues, or at least some of them, is the purpose of the following analysis.

Our task is to investigate the value-consciousness of Israeli society against the background of the period since the establishment of the State of Israel. We shall begin with a statement about the positions of values vis-à-vis individuals and groups of people. Underlying our discussion is the assumption about the objective validity of values. In other words, values do not change. What does change is the awareness of values, their impact on those who respond to them, and the situation in which they should be realized.

One of the pivotal points in the changing character of value-awareness versus the nonchanging position of values is the selection performed by individuals. An example in the personal sphere is when a teacher is guided by adherence to strict discipline rather than to a good-natured tolerance in his daily work in the classroom. The teacher selects from a reservoir of values of a particular guiding principle of behavior. In turn, we may ask about the particular motivation expressed in this particular selection: was it a matter of temperament or an evaluating of the situation, or the result of understanding the pupil's character? A similar analysis applies to groups of people. When people activate the value of self-expression—or the value of unity and solidarity—this too can be subjected to an investigation of the background and the motivation for adherence to one value as opposed to another.

For the sake of our present investigation, it is enough to point out the distinction between values and their impact, by emphasizing the close relation between impact and the selection of values. It follows that a closer look at the value-consciousness of Israeli society will disclose the changing patterns of selection between different principles of action and behavior. This requires one qualification: that we assume the distinction between value and value-consciousness, although in the context of the following analysis, this statement may sound more like a credo than the outcome of fully developed reflection. With this reservation, we may embark on our task.[1]

※ ※ ※

We may consider the value-consciousness of Israeli society through a retrospective comparison with the set of values that guided the pre-state society, the Yishuv. The ordinary patterns of societal organization cannot be applied to this society. It was not a native society but one of immigrants, reinforced by a perpetual flow of newcomers. It was not a tribal society, subject to a colonial regime. The society of the Yishuv was in fact a "proto-state" under a proto-government of semi-governmental Jewish institutions.

The maintenance of this proto-state depended largely on a strong sense of purpose. This sense activated large groups of individuals who formulated the ethos of society at large. With this sense of purpose came a feeling of solidarity, which in turn was probably rooted on a vague prevailing feeling that Jews make a single family despite heir frictions—and these were many. The solidarity, as it supported the sense of purpose, absorbed also its effects. Solidarity not only expresses a sense of belonging characteristic of members of one family, it has also a functional validity. The goals of society cannot be achieved without solidarity. The attempts to overcome the difficulties of the minority status of the Yishuv, together with the tensions between the Yishuv and the Arab world surrounding it and the British mandatory power could not have succeeded without the conviction that strength lay in unity. Solidarity was paradigmatic of the mood of the pre-state society. The motivating factors in this mood operated both on a basic level and on a functional one. Each of these levels reinforced the other.

In retrospect it is important to point out the permeation of national aspirations by a social consciousness. To use Zionist terminology, the social aspects came under "productivization," that is, the restructuring of the professions Jews were engaged in historically. It meant establishing the base of a socioeconomic pyramid by transforming many Jews into urban manual laborers or agriculture workers. Manual labor was considered to be the source of human activity, a link between man and the world. It meant the recovery of those skills and abilities in the Jewish people, lost to them through many years of engaging in commerce and liberal professions. Agriculture was viewed not only as the root of all economic activity, but as man's root in the land. Through agriculture people could become not only the owners of land but also "the salt of the earth."

We may point out an additional factor in the structure and climate of proto-state society: the sense of isolation, which, to a very large extent, was active in one creation of the society's *esprit de corps.* The feeling of standing alone is a kind of legacy of the memorial experience of the Jews and it was reinforced in the course of the history of Yishuv society. The Balfour declaration of 1917 was viewed, by and large, as a triumphant installation of the Jews on the main track of Western societies. But the many disillusions that followed the declaration enhanced the need for self-reliance, which, in turn, activated a sense of isolation. As we have pointed out before, Zionism carried a built-in propensity to self-emancipation, to achievement by one's own efforts. Unfulfilled hope reactivated the notion of self-emancipation. The Holocaust of European Jewry, which happened a few years prior to the establishment of the State of Israel became a powerful factor in nourishing the Yishuv's sense of isolation and facilitated the development of the sense of solidarity.

In addressing ourselves to values and their impact, we may be tempted to draw too rosy a picture, stressing values and value-awareness and disregarding problems, strife, and defiance of values. Yishuv society obviously had communal problems. Before the towns developed into metropolitan areas, they already had slums. Thus, in addition to the impact of value-awareness, various social factors were operating in Yishuv society. This led to the usual clash between the impact of these factors and the controlling values of the society. There is also a quantitative difference between pre-state and state society. The underprivileged have become more visible: quantity has been transformed into quality. When social problems emerge against a background of independence, the sense of guilt and impotence increases. There is no third party to blame.

※ ※ ※

There is also a continuity between the pre-state situation and that in the State of Israel, in spite of the obvious transformations. That continuity is related to the sense of isolation characteristic of Israeli society, to the persistence of the feeling of solidarity possibly rooted in some unconscious layer of Jewish experience as well as in the constant exposure to hostility, and, lastly, in a sense of purpose. This last aspect points to a paradox in the moral and psychological texture of Israeli society and to some of its problems.

Indeed, the establishment of the State of Israel is a paramount achievement. Therefore it poses the question of how to maintain the feeling of achievement without relaxing and without changing the attitude and the meaning of the society. Pioneers, as we know from social history, are inclined to look at their pioneering as historically determined—that is, related to particular and thus, changing, conditions. One of the major problems facing Israeli society is to maintain a pioneering attitude in new conditions, to acknowledge novelty and to promote the sense that this novelty is not only the end of a period but a new beginning.

From a different point of view, a pioneering attitude is not only a matter of daring, of frontiers, or of venturing into unknown areas. It involves a preference for social goals over one's personal achievement in terms of economic and financial rewards. Hence, between rights and duties, the pioneering society is inclined to lay the emphasis on duties. It is meritorious to forego personal benefits for the sake of social values.

The establishment of the State of Israel did not change the balance between rights and duties, but gave them an institutional manifestation.[2] The State of Israel assigns primacy to defense considerations, that is to say, to considerations that are, by definitions, of an all-embracing character related to society and not to the individuals constituting it. The needs of defense call up every citizen to the army. The forces are made up of conscripts and a hard core of career officers, the bulk being reservists. There is a continuous flow of civilians into the army and conversely, returning to civilian life. All this does not involve voluntary decision but is part of the compulsory character of statehood. Duty is now institutionalized. It is no longer grounded in personal decision, for it is safeguarded by legal sanctions.

The characteristic tension between different values and attitudes in one's own psyche becomes depersonalized or objectivized. Duties transplanted to the public realm become separated from personal decisions and inclinations. The personal sphere ceases to be exposed to a particular kind of social tension and becomes an oasis where one's private rights are to be safeguarded and enjoyed. The objectivization of duties creates an urge for reward on the personal level.

This trend has been enhanced by the economic development and technological growth of Israeli society, especially since the 1967 "Six Days War." There is a difference between growth for the sake of reinforcing society and its independence, and growth for the sake of raising individual standards of living. It is rather difficult and perhaps even impossible to separate the two aspects of economic growth, that is, the strengthening of the texture of economic activities and the raising of individual standards of living.

Although one can argue that serving the goals of society is an end in itself, it is difficult to argue that economic growth is an end in itself. That growth, dependent on the processes of production and consumption, carries in itself the objective of production. Consumption relates eventually to living human beings, while production can be anonymous. Even when it is impossible to distinguish between duties and rights, the emphasis on economic growth is bound to have a significant impact on the value-awareness of society. While society professes a preponderance of public goals, economic growth creates a preponderance of personal benefits. One of the major problems of Israeli society lies precisely in the discrepancy between the embracing framework and the economic core identical with consumption. Israel faces the problems of not being "a consumer society" let alone guided by consumer culture.

※ ※ ※

This discrepancy is reinforced by the emphasis on economic growth, which tends to evoke an accelerated pace. People are tested by their ability to go along with the process and to fulfill the functions imposed by it. The emphasis on professional education, on innovation, on managerial talent, introduces into Israeli society dynamics characteristic of the Western world. But in Israel those dynamics operate in a society that consists of many new immigrants. They came to Israel to find a homeland and they are faced with the problems of social and economic development characteristic of society in general. Many of those in Israel who experience Western society and its problems are Jews from North African and other Moslem countries. They are, according to their origins, members of communities still carrying on their own traditions, and using their inherited structures as a form of psychological self-defense. Economic growth and improved standards of living, which affect everybody in the society, do not necessarily lead to equality. Sometimes the gap between the different social strata widens: in Israel, this development has an additional meaning related to the national and ideological ethos of the society. In the first place, the nonegalitarian situation clashes with the feeling of solidarity to which we have referred. Those motivated by solidarity are more willing to try to mitigate the nonegalitarian situation. They are aware of the contradiction between solidarity as an ideological credo and the overt denial of solidarity. Israel carries within itself the experience of the Diaspora, which declares that inflictions on the Jews are due to persecution by the outside world. Hence Jews left to themselves should be able to find their way. Yet this notion is inhibited by the nonegalitarian situation prevailing in Israel. Jews among themselves must either struggle for the removal of social obstacles, or else they must admit that not everybody is originally endowed with the power of social mobility or with the ability to keep up with the development of society.

A distinction must be maintained between economic growth and over-emphasis on economic growth, or even between affluence and luxury. A controlled rate of growth can prevent a clash between social orientation and the search for personal benefits: or, at least, it may prevent a widening of the gap between the two goals. This calls for an evaluation of the real needs of society, though it is difficult to determine what is real and what is spurious. There is also the interdependence between economic growth and nonegalitarianism. Socioeconomic investment has to be concentrated on those who have not yet reached a certain level. That level does not imply only income and housing, but also flexibility, vitality, self-reliance, and initiative. The discrepancy between different strata of the population requires an educational ethos that will address itself differently to different people, while maintaining an identity of attitude and a single value-consciousness. The egalitarian spirit will lead to different practical policies. Those exposed to the predicaments of economic growth and not to its benefits should be considered as requiring special treatment. This involves the infusion of virtues that have become less important to those who already enjoy the fruits of economic development. To put it like this: there is a difference between the attitude toward food of people who are hungry and those who tend to overeat. To refrain from overeating is perhaps an imposition in so far as one's urges and inclinations are concerned: but it is grounded all the same in a concern for the person. It appeals to one's better self as against one's egoism. Here is one of the major crossroads of contemporary Israeli society as far as motivation by values is implied.

※ ※ ※

The value-awareness so far discussed is intrinsically connected with values of an ethical character, such as solidarity and equality. We must now consider the clash between a technological civilization and its impact on Israeli society and the *raison d'etre* of Israel's cultural renaissance. The interaction between these two cultural and intellectual trends is not entirely detached from the aspect previously discussed, since the problems pertaining to the egalitarian outlook are reinforced by technological and economic developments. But questions referring to technological culture cannot be simply subsumed under ethical considerations, because technological society is a broader and more empirical frame of reference than that delineated by ethical values in the strict sense of the term.

For our present purpose, it is not necessary to attempt to outline the full implications of technological civilization. It is enough to say that it derives its momentum, in the first place, from the urge to conquer nature and the world and to control them. Second, it creates an overriding intellectual climate in which human attitudes amount to human tasks: the challenging tasks are those for which workable methods have not yet been devised. It is because of the centrality of tasks and problems to be solved that technological civilization creates a future-oriented society, a society directed toward the time when the solutions will eventually be found.

Future-orientedness creates, as a by-product, the rhythm of technological civilization and of the society shaped by it. It is now fashionable to criticize the waste characteristic of this civilization. But it is not only a question of waste; we are really facing deliberate oblivion. Many things produced, and also many values, are regarded as obsolete simply because they were created or formulated in the past. They belong to the realm of that which exists already and by definition are not to be located in the dimension of the future.

For the purpose of this analysis, it will suffice to point out that renaissance is by definition past-oriented, even when its essential aim is to rejuvenate the past or reformulate it, rather than simply repeat or even reconstitute it. Whatever applies to the problematic situation of any renaissance movement applies equally to the various trends of the Jewish renaissance and to the underlying motivation of the creation of a Jewish state and an independent Jewish society. However, the decisive period in the Jewish renewal movement did not occur in a historically minded atmosphere. Zionism, though conceived in the nineteenth century, reached materialization and its "moment of truth" in the twentieth century, at the peak of technological civilization. Hence, we cannot avoid the clash between the future-consciousness of technological impact and the attachment to the past, which is essential to the renaissance trend, however it is interpreted.

It is easier to analyze the situation than to envisage a way out of it, or at least a *modus vivendi* between the two trends. What can be said is that perhaps Israeli society, or some part of it, is aware that the chaotic clash between the trends does not create a cohesive cultural milieu. At the same time, there are signs of a growing awareness that technology alone cannot create the infrastructure of a society. A civilization dependent on perpetual mobility lacks the elements of constancy and permanence essential for social cohesion. As we have said before, that situation and problems involved are inherent in Israeli society. No harmonious solution can be envisaged.

※ ※ ※

Israeli society is a minority surrounded by a world that differs from it in culture and religion. This difference is expressed in a hostile attitude. Israeli society is constantly being reminded of its difference, and forced to redefine its differences and its causes. These lie in the historical continuity of the Jewish people and in the attachment of the society to the origins of its existence.

Every once in a while, a new factor emerges. For instance, there is the impact of Soviet Jewry on the Jewish people as a whole and on Israeli society in particular. The human right to leave a country has become involved with the right of the Jews to go to the country that they consider their homeland. This brings home to Israel the universal Jewish dimension of its existence. That dimension contains not only the sociodemographic but also the cultural-historical aspect. Together they create a problem but they also help to keep the renaissance aspect alive.

The cultural renaissance cannot be restricted to the historical dimension. After all, the historical culture of the Jewish people is a religious culture, and with all its variations there never was a nonreligious Jewish culture. Hence the issue of the renaissance compels us to consider the question of religion. During two thousand years of Diaspora existence the Jewish religion did not develop ways and means of coping with two elements in the modern situation: technological civilization and Jewish social and political independence. The contemporary Jewish cultural renaissance therefore has to work within the sphere of the Jewish religion, its concepts and attitudes.

Possibly the factor that gave rise to that renaissance—and this in itself is a paradox—came from culturally and intellectually motivated circles whose basic loyalty is of a nonreligious character or at least of a nontraditional character. These people, in a way, are raising the problem. Whether they can find a solution or whether the solution will be formulated by those who are primarily religious and take a traditional stand—that is one of the questions to be faced by Israeli society.

Right now it is only possible to say that what is characteristic of the Israelis is a visible disequilibrium between overwhelming problems of an intellectual and cultural character and the inadequacy of the solutions available. This disequilibrium in turn can be a very strong motivating force in social and cultural trends, but it can also be a weakening factor. Both ways are open and as the biblical saying has it, "choose life."

It would be presumptuous to assert that a solution has been found to the dilemmas we have analyzed. However, the technological dilemma is to some extent more easily dealt with than the cultural one. It will take of course a great deal of motivation, persistence, and tenacity to solve the technological problem. But since it has institutional expressions, it is as a matter of principle solvable, if not totally, then by way of pointing out a direction. The cultural dilemma, grounded in the renaissance aspect of Israeli society, has to rely on convictions and their impact on attitudes and emotions. No legislation can possibly solve that problem or mitigate it. Here we must address curatives to a *Weltanschauung* proper. The only possible approach now is to maintain a kind of eclectic attitude simultaneously combining different convictions, not suppressing them but letting them mold life—at a time when cultural and educational decisions cannot be postponed any more.

The two areas discussed show some similarity, since the question of a viable synthesis affects them both as a major issue. The first synthesis is that if a technological society and its economic repercussions, on the one hand, and the value of human concern and equality on the other. The second is that of technological civilization and its impact on the renaissance factor of Zionism and the State of Israel. There remains the question of a possible synthesis between the two directions. As usual in these explorations, one man's synthesis is the other man's compromise.

※ ※ ※

The third cluster of problems deals with the impact of defense and security considerations on the character of Israeli society. Observers, mainly outside Israel, consider this the most important question. Many an observer, even those motivated by understanding and good will, expresses the fear that Israeli society is drifting in the direction of modern Sparta, motivated not only by actual security needs but developing into a society awarding priority to military virtues, monolithic solidarity, and its implications.

There is no need to make this argument more explicit, since we have already employed the most striking and frightening association, Sparta, which of course involves the spirit of Sparta and the traditional juxtaposition with Athens. Though the value-concern is related by a desired synthesis, one can say at this juncture that somehow a working synthesis has been found between military and defense considerations on the one hand and the full spectrum of human activities on the other—whether we assume that there is a deliberate search for such synthesis or we state that factually things are like that.

Any description of the life of Israeli society is bound to speak of the variety of activities in the social, cultural, artistic, and intellectual spheres in addition to, or besides, the prominence of military achievements and defense technology. One can easily argue that in this diversity of activities a sense for life and for "good life" is manifest. Or else, one can argue that there are so many problems bewildering Israeli society that merely the urge for survival dictates that society is bound to find channels to express the latent abilities of the diversity of people composing it.

As an example, let us point out one significant line of activity in science and scholarship. In addition to the common motivating factors (talent, curiosity, etc.) there is also another factor operating consciously and unconsciously in Israeli society. For various reasons Jews have excelled in scholarship over generations, that is, scholarship applied to the sources of Jewish tradition. Since the emancipation Jews have excelled in scholarship and in science, applying themselves not only to their own history, but to the problems of the world and of diverse historical and literary sources and traditions. Israeli society, representing the totality of the Jewish people, is somehow driven by the urge or aspiration to live up to the standards its predecessors reached in the past. This might be one explanation why in spite of the fact that so many talents are active in the military area, there is enough talent left for other spheres of activity related not only to "mere" life but to "good" life.

There is probably an additional cause for the synthesis or *modus vivendi* with regard to the impact of security and objectives. Israeli society is vividly aware of being encircled by enemies. Many people wrongly expect a simple response to a simple stimulus, but fortunately things are not that simple. In a situation of encirclement relatively small groups will develop a sense that quality has to compensate for quantity, since there are no prospects of achieving equality on the level of quantity. That connotes, even in the context of military considerations, not only courage, readiness to die, etc., but also self-reliance, initiative, alertness, and the kind of individual performance that is not swallowed up by units, collectives, brigades, etc. Perhaps we face here a paradox when we compare the situation in Israel with the usual concept of military excellence and its emphasis on group performance. In Israel a situation has developed where precisely for the sake of military achievement, it is not enough to rely on the cohesion and discipline of groups.

Hence Israel's military structure stresses the virtues and values of friendship and camaraderie among soldiers. These virtues most prominently epitomize the nonmilitary virtues; that is, the human and the civilian. Be that as it may, the facts do not corroborate the cliché of militarism and probably should not be a source for such concern in the future. This does not mean to say that there are no problems in that sphere, but possibly not in the direction expressed by the fear of an overmilitarization of Israeli society.

We have dealt with the atmosphere of Israeli society and its impact on the army. These observations should be supplemented by an additional one, on the attitude of people enlisted and the principles prevailing among them. One must be mentioned specifically. It is known in Hebrew as *Tohar Ha-Neshek* (the purity of weapons). That principle, like many moral norms, can perhaps best be formulated negatively: to not employ weapons except in situations where it is necessary and unavoidable. It is clear that the evaluation of any concrete situation in which that principle has to be applied rests ultimately with the officers or even with the individual soldiers. Hence the application of the principle to a concrete situation can be disputable and mistakes can occur. But the principle in its abstract form creates at least an initial hesitation, and consequently views the employment of weapons as an *ultima ratio* only. This principle was probably formulated against the background of Israeli society where a distinction prevails between hostilities and wars as a necessity, a bad one at that, and a positive evaluation of war as a display of heroism and devotion. The principle of *Tohar Ha-Neshek* expresses this distinction. Israeli society attempts—and this is a deliberately mitigating proposition—to evoke loyalty and devotion in spite of the basic rejection of war. This rejection is implied in the evaluation of war as a necessity and not as a state of euphoria. The atmosphere of living in a situation of siege is—at least to some extent—neutralized or mitigated by the very vivid public opinion expressed in the media. The mitigated trend is strongly reinforced by the status of the judicial system of Israel and the very high authority and esteem of the Supreme court.

Having said this, we come back to our previous point, that the assessment of one area in life as not being strongly exposed to problems cannot overshadow the fact that other areas are afflicted with very serious difficulties. After dealing with the climate of opinion of Israeli society, we return to the ideological approach in its pronounced mode.

Notes

1. For a discussion of some structural aspects of the social and political realm see: Nathan Rotenstreich, *Order and Might*. State University of New York Press, 1988.

2. Rights and duties are analyzed in the above mentioned book, p. 209.

Chapter 6

Toward a Reformulation of Zionist Ideology

The previous chapters were concerned with an analysis of some trends inherent in Zionism. We now turn to the major issue of contemporary Zionism for which the essential point is its reformulation.

The point of departure of the following analysis is that there is no Zionist ideology today. In seeking to explain this condition, we cannot make use of the well-known claim that we live in a post-ideological era. Our task is to ask more specific questions related to the Jewish situation as we experience it. This situation is characterized by two elements: the existence of the State of Israel and the shift of world Jewry to the American continent. These two elements must be seen not as dependent on each other, but as coexistent.

The existence of the State of Israel can explain the disappearance of the Zionist ideology insofar as any realization of a broad social-political goal may make the guiding ideology obsolete. Obviously the emergence of the State of Israel has been grounded in the Zionist ideology. Hence, the question of the connection between the ideology and its realization is bound to be a central issue in present-day Jewish awareness. Zionist ideology has a special character, which makes it different from the ideologies of other national movements. Zionist ideology, aiming to establish an independent Jewish entity, has not been part of an existing society aspiring to express its existence in the reality of its state. It has belonged to the Jewish people living in the Diaspora, outside the boundaries of the projected political entity. Hence, it is a national movement of return—to emphasize it again—not one aiming to establish a correlation between a given social infrastructure and a political structure. Zionism has not been based on the desire to achieve continuity between the social existence of a people and its manifestation in statehood. It has been based on an attempt to create both the social groundwork and its political manifestation.

Aspirations for independence have been related to a central issue in classical Zionist ideology, namely an analysis of the situation of the Jewish people in the Diaspora particularly since the nineteenth century. To identify the essence of that classical ideology, it is appropriate to follow some of the distinctions made in the formulation of that ideology. We observe the distinction between what has been called the question of the Jews and the question of Judaism. In a controversy between Ahad Ha'am and Herzl, the former was more realistic—in viewing the situation in the contemporary era—than Herzl. We adhere to these distinctions not because of nostalgia but because they contain some relevant points, which may direct us in dealing with the situation of the Jews today. The question of the Jews is based on their exposure to persecution and rejection. The question of Judaism is based on the existence of its cultural cohesion.

We referred before to these two conceptions. Now we shall summarize them as they may serve as a proper point of departure of the contemporary situation, not only as a historical background.

The concern with the condition of the Jews began because Jews lived among and depended on the peoples of the world. This dependence found its concrete expression in persecution, rejection, and generally speaking, the failure of even the modern, legally constituted state, to absorb the Jews without distinguishing between them and their environment. It is appropriate to mention that Herzl, who so sharply analyzed the realities of the Jewish situation, clung to Lessing's idea of the education of mankind. He adheres to the historical aim that reality as it is fell short of that goal.

Empirical, that is to say historical, reality leads to disappointment in emancipation, or to the loss of hope that emancipation will achieve its goal in the foreseeable future. Hence, against the background of persecutions and the tensions that go with them, the solution was proposed, that Jews withdraw from day-to-day social and political relations and move toward independence. Jews in that framework of independence will be released from the continuous tension between them and their environment. Thus, independence and its political expression as a state of the Jews is a solution based on the withdrawal of the Jews from the network of relations with their environment. Independence is by definition the opposite of encroachment on the life of the Jews.

Against this view, Ahad Ha'am formulated a position that he himself called an analysis of the problem of Judaism and that we can perhaps now call the problem of Jewishness. Ahad Ha'am distinguished between the question of the Jews and the question of Judaism. He argued, among other things, that the question of the Jews cannot be solved. Jews are bound always to live among the nations of the world and suffer the difficulties of that existence. Hence, he emphasized the question of Judaism that was tantamount to the contraction of the national ego, that is, the collective Jewish existence, which, among other things, is also a cultural entity promoting the creativity of the Jewish people in pursuing its own tradition, beliefs, and orientations.

In the modern era that creativity has been exposed to a persistent limitation, since the Jews cannot maintain what we would now call their cultural identity. This is so because they are so strongly influenced by the surrounding world that their own creativity is progressively diminishing. Ahad Ha'am did not deny the persecution of the Jews, but he pointed out that within the situation of life in exile there is an ongoing absorption of the influences from the non-Jewish world. The first component of the situation—persecution—cannot be negated, but an attempt should be made to confront the second component—of diminished and diminishing identity—aiming at strengthening the creativity of the Jewish people that is so crucial also for resisting external forces.

Ahad Ha'am pointed out that not only was Jewish creativity diminishing, but also the impact of the Jewish tradition on the Jews was becoming more and more limited. Hence, Ahad Ha'am represents the trend to withdraw from the circle of the influencing environment, not in order to gain release from the pressure, but in order to reinforce the standing of the Jewish people on its own and within its own historical boundaries.

※ ※ ※

Retrospectively, we can say that the two trends, despite the clash between them, prompted the conception of the independence of the Jewish people, regardless of the interpretation of independence. The central issue in this context is that the different formulations emerged within the settings of central and eastern European Jewry. These formulations were attempts to analyze the situation of the Jews in Europe before World War I and of course World War II. With the establishment of the State of Israel a new context for the question of the Jews, as well as the question of Judaism, emerges. The center of gravity of the Jewish people shifted from Europe to the United States (outside of the state of Israel).

The catastrophe that befell European Jewry was not the cause of the shift, but historically or retrospectively, the two events have to be seen in one context. The question facing Zionist ideology today is: Are the two orientations of the classical ideology valid for the Jews in the United States? As a matter of fact, Zionism as an ideology and as a movement directed by that ideology is dependent on this issue. To put it negatively: Is there room for a new approach to Jewish reality, which is not a repetition of the classical views? We refer mainly to the Jews of North America, though we cannot be oblivious to the differences between their position and that of the Jews in South America or the Soviet Union before its dissolution and after it.

※ ※ ※

The characteristic essence of the present-day Jewish reality is mainly that the tension caused by persecution, which was a constant feature of the situation of the Jews in Europe and which found its expression in Zionist analysis, no longer exists. Jews attained human rights expressed not only in political and legal equality, but also in equality in terms of social mobility.

Jews became emancipated but not through their own struggle for their position within society and the state. Emancipation was granted them as a consequence of the processes of the society, the legal system, and the structure of the state. The Jews *got* emancipation: they did not *achieve* it by way of their own struggle.

Hence, within the self-consciousness of the Jews, we find not even a vestige of their struggle for themselves. This enhances the absence of tension between the Jews and their environment. The characteristic features of the classical Jewish question do not exist anymore. In any case, we cannot point to the Jewish predicament as it has been conceived in its classical analysis. The Jewish question, in the classical sense of that term, found its solution without taking steps to withdraw from the environment; on the contrary, it was solved by growing roots in the environment.

As a matter of fact, there is no longer any difference between the Jews and their environment. In the major day-to-day activities of the Jews, we cannot point to any barrier between them and their environment. This is so even though here and there, people refer to a latent anti-Semitism in the United States. The reference is to *latent* anti-Semitism. If such anti-Semitism exists, it is not a feature of the regime nor of the mood and trends of the society at large. In this sense, the phenomenon of assimilation has changed: Jews do not assimilate *into* the environment, they are part of it. In any case, an attempt to revitalize Zionist ideology cannot be based on "the Jewish question" because there is no such question and certainly not a sharp one.

How do things stand from the perspective of the question of Judaism? Here, too, for different reasons, we have to conclude that that question does not exist either. This is so, since as we have seen that question has been put forward against the background of the creativity of the Jewish people as a collective entity. In addition, for this question to be central we must assume that the Jewish people want to maintain its cultural creativity within its own boundaries, and that it does not consciously and deliberately identify itself with the environment, that it does not want to absorb the environment, even when exposed to its impact.

But when the Jews become an integral part of the environment, they do not look for the breadth and depth of Jewish creativity, even when this or that Jewish author can be interpreted as being prompted by Jewish motives. The first social aspect of involvement in the environment leads to the second aspect, namely the assimilation of intellectual trends prevailing in the comprehensive civilization. This is so to a large extent because of the major change in the broad reading of the contemporary world.

The encounter is no longer with historical or religious traditions, as was the case in Europe, with the tension being largely a religious one or at least rooted in it. The contemporary encounter is with a universal culture or with a universal civilization that is scientific and technological; as such it puts aside historical and religious conceptions. As long as religious conceptions were present, universal civilization could not be the dominant factor. In the change that occurred, the religious component becomes secondary and the scientific and technological climate of opinion becomes central. The historical differences do not have an impact any more on the present-day situation.

Previously, Jews and Judaism faced traditional societies and cultures grounded in religions as a sum total of articles of faith and modes of behavior. Hence, Jews were continuously aware of their unwavering adherence to their own tradition even without being reminded of it. The situation in the contemporary period is essentially different, since the surrounding culture and the society it guides, being scientific and technological, is no longer shaped by traditional components. For that society tradition is at most a reservoir of vestiges of the past. This applies both to the surrounding society and to Jewish existence. Though Jews may want to maintain their loyalty to their history they are bound to place it at the margin of their existence, since they adhere to society at large and are not at all willing to forego that adherence. Hence, they demonstrate their Jewish loyalty not in faith and ways of life but in sentiments and organizations shaped by it that are mainly of a ceremonial character.

※ ※ ※

This is a new situation, which classical Zionism could not foresee. Hence, the concern with the situation of the Jewish people in our generation, even against the background of the existence of the state of Israel, is bound to refer to a different, essentially new reality. Therefore, we must ask: Is there a Jewish question, or is it a question of Judaism, or is there a new combination of the two classical approaches to the situation of the Jewish people because of the new situation? The major characteristic feature of the Jewish situation in the open contemporary society is that there is no public Jewish realm or Jewish commonwealth. The interaction between Jews is mundane and is based not on common ground, but again on some vestiges of the past which are marginal to the involvement in the surrounding society. To be sure, European Jewry did not and could not maintain a public Jewish realm, because of the situation in exile (*Golah*). Still, there existed a community or communality based on common modes of daily behavior. This comprehensive Jewish way of life brought Jews to one another. In a situation where there is no infrastructure of such a communality, those components of reality, which are not part of the surrounding society, become scattered vestiges of an adherence to that which existed before. Communality is not a comprehensive background for Jewish existence, but is relegated to the margins of the society at large. Jews are at least superficially loyal to the vestiges because they want something particular of their own that does not encroach on the comprehensive mode of existence.

If there could be, and should be, an attempt to anchor a new conception of Zionism in the reality as it is, it is essential to emphasize that component of a common Jewish reality. The conclusion is bound to be that such a common framework of reality is impossible in the situation of an open society. That which was characteristic of the classical aspiration to achieve Jewish independence—the search for a resolution of the problem of persecutions—must become the search for a new mode of Jewish existence. Independence becomes coterminous with the Jewish common reality. It is positive in its essence and not a response to rejection.

This is the issue before us. It has to be said that Zionism, after the emergence of the State of Israel did not address itself to this issue. On the contrary, we witness the disappearance of an ideological approach founded in self-examination. It has been replaced by a continuous attempt to safeguard support for the State of Israel. That support is appealing mainly to the Jewish feeling of solidarity and that solidarity leads to continuous attempts to find a focus for Jewish comprehensive existence. Since that focus cannot be present in the day-to-day existence of the Jews in the Diaspora, it is shifted outside it, beyond it, that is to say, to the State of Israel, as exemplifying the unity of the Jewish people and making it symbolically manifest.

※ ※ ※

At this juncture, we ask a theoretical question, which is not confined only to the Jewish situation: What is the significance of a public realm in human existence? The public realm is not only the meeting ground of individuals or groups. That realm not only enables the meeting between people, it also shapes a certain mode of existence, which by definition is beyond the activity of any individual person, however creative he may be. One of the basic manifestations of the public realm is the common language that serves as a background against which individual activity makes shape. The public realm is not only a ground for encounters, but also for communalities, which become manifest in institutions or in the law.

Sometimes that common sphere is not defined. In any case there is a continuous interaction between the individual existence and that which is beyond the individuals. In this sense, the public realm is one expression of the transpersonal component of human reality. The normative aspect of the public realm is but the other side of that transpersonal component. The transpersonal component is manifest even in the compulsion inherent in the public realm. Compulsion is a kind of equivalent or surrogate ensuring that individuals will go beyond themselves even when their intentions do not spontaneously lead them in that direction.

In any case, the significance of the public realm as the communality of the Jews is a major issue for Jewish existence today. That issue should be the point of departure for a new Zionist conception—a conception that does not yet exist. We must observe that not only does such a conception not exist but also that many of the analyses by Jews in the United States are rather self-satisfied and do not address the problem of the comprehensive shape of Jewish existence. The undeniable achievements of American Jewry do not indicate that the present situation contains the possibilities of common Jewish existence. The analysis must look to the future and not merely compare what the Jews have achieved today with what they had or enjoyed in previous generations.

The analysis of the possible components of the reformulation of the Zionist ideology has concentrated on the ideology within the context of the Diaspora. This has been prescribed by the inherent trend of Zionism to negate the Diaspora in the sense dealt with before. Zionism as an ideology is directed toward the situation as it is shaped and to build a new mode of Jewish existence, and that demand is directed toward the Jewry living in the Diaspora.

※ ※ ※

Still, there is the question of the impact of ideology on the existence of Israeli society. Is the realization of the ideology a release from the commitment to it? What mode of synthesis between the involvement in Israeli society and the commitment to the Jewish people will take place? There is more of a sociopsychological analysis of the people of the society than an ideological formulation. Israel seems to be satisfied with its support as a visible feature of Diaspora Jewry and here the component of support, which seems to be sufficient for the bulk of Western Jewry is accepted by Israel and by the Jews in the West. Still, some issues cannot be left to the process without the intervention of an ideological approach. We shall touch on some basic topics.

In this context, the situation after the Six-Day War is rather significant. It can therefore be said that the impact of the Six-Day

War expressed itself in an attempt to bring together the historical dimension of Zionism with Messianic expectation, which has been interpreted as relating to territorial sovereignty. At the same time, the holiness of the Land of Israel has been interpreted as related to the space of this land and not intrinsically to the modes of life of human beings—that is, of the Jewish population within the state.

From the point of view of historical research, the question is still open as to the relation or comparison of Messianic expectations to the fundamental trend of Zionism, namely whether Zionism replaced Messianism or whether it is a particular interpretation of it. But what has occurred since the Six-Day War has been an attempt to materialize or realize Messianism within the boundaries of Zionism, interpreting the extension of the sovereignty of the State of Israel—to say the least—as a move toward the Messianic fulfillment. Sovereignty, from the negative point of view, is the overcoming of submission to the gentile world, and has been understood both as a realization of the Zionist expectation and as a realization of Messianism.

Zionism, at least in some of its trends, was concerned with an attempt to establish an integrated society expressing itself in the political realm. Indeed, this applies to parts of Israeli society.

In the wake of the Six-Day War, the territorial and political aspects become isolated from the integrated approach to Jewish reality, as if the political component could be self-sufficient. The problem of ruling over the Arab population was thereby confronted without considering that the extension of sovereignty implied such rule and the problems related to it. Instead of looking at statehood as expressing human reality, statehood has been viewed as occupying an independent or even self-enclosed status.

When we look at this development from a broader point of view, two aspects have to be mentioned. In the first place, we can consider Zionism in its classical shape as being characterized by a synthesis—though such a synthesis is always volatile—between a utopian aspiration and a pragmatic approach to day-to-day reality. This synthesis led Zionism to many of its achievements. The utopian expectation, inherent in the very return to the Land of Israel, did not overshadow the various attempts to take advantage of the processes of reality and the possibilities or opportunities, which these processes brought to the fore, and provided the Zionist aspiration with the means whereby it could be realized in a piecemeal way. After the Six-Day War, the utopian component became detached both ideologically and practically from the pragmatic one. To put it in a different way, the pragmatic component is no longer a significant part of a synthesis between utopia and practicality. At the center of the dissolution of the synthesis lies the interpretation of statehood and sovereignty, replacing the interpretation of the relations between the populous and the political realm.

A second aspect concerns the impact of moral considerations on pragmatic ones. The negation or the denial of the rights of the Jewish people, which has been the major motivation of the Arab world in its hostility to Israel, should not lead to a denial of moral considerations in the Jewish encounter with the Arab world. The negation of the Jews, either practically or ideologically, also became the focal point of Arab nationalism, at least of the Palestinian variety. What Herzl remarked about a people—it exists as an entity because of a common enemy—became paradoxically the focal point of Palestinian nationalism. The Palestinians consider themselves as a national entity expressed in their rejection of Zionism and the State of Israel. That awareness grew with the process of opposition to Zionism and to the Jewish entity embodied in the State of Israel.

The lack of awareness of these aspects of both ideological points of consideration and day-to-day reality became a negative feature of Zionism after the Six-Day War. One could say that Zionism has been swept up by day-to-day reality, without consideration given to principles and ideas. But being swept up by that reality brings about a situation in which one is not in a position to guide and direct it toward one's goals.

There is one element in the context of the complexities of the relations between the society of Israel and American Jewry, which becomes prominent from time to time. That element is connected to the fact that American Jews as individuals or bodies of American Jewry, express their opinions on controversial topics of the Israeli political position vis-à-vis the Arabs, the situation in the occupied territories, and the outbreak of the Intifada in recent years. The critical expressions of American Jews are sometimes rejected by Israeli political leaders, whereby the main argument against those expressions is that those who are not involved in the Israeli situation and do not carry the burden of the security problems, should refrain from expressing their views because of the security situation. It is warranted to assume that that position taken by political leaders is a direct or indirect attempt to prevent critical expression. The argument of referring to the day-to-day existence of American Jews, which differs from the exposure to dangers of the Israeli citizen, is politically motivated.

Against any argument of this sort, the ideological consideration should prevail. If Israel is a state of the Jewish people and not only of the Jews living in Israel, one can not hamper the expression of views related to the situation of Israel and the political directions guiding it. The ideological perspective should be dominant even when one assumes clashes of orientation.

It is obvious that the Jews in America are sensitive to the status of a national minority and transpose their sensitivity to the situation in Israel and its encounter with Arabs. Jews in America are impressed by the attitudes of official policy of the American government and the public opinion in America. These empirical aspects cannot make Israelis oblivious to American Jewry inherent ideological commitment.

By and large, the same consideration applies to the internal situation of Israel. For instance, the religious structure in Israel, which grants unequivocally primacy to the Orthodox orientation. This is an on going issue in the relations between the Jewish state and the largest Jewish community outside of it

A reformulation of the Zionist ideology presupposes a self-analysis of the Jewish situation in the present. Ahad Ha'am's conception of the concentration of the Jewish national ego looms large in that analysis, whether consciously or not. The demographic component and its future prognosis should also be central in this reformulation.

Afterword

SHLOMO AVINERI

This volume is obviously a torso, and had Nathan Rotenstreich lived to see the last few years' developments in Israel and the Middle East, he would certainly have addressed the intellectual consequences of the three most dramatic events of the period: the opportunity for a historical compromise between Israelis and Palestinians heralded by the Oslo accords, the assassination of Prime Minister Yitzhak Rabin by an anti-Oslo nationalist-religious Jewish student and the following election victory of Benjamin Netanyahu's Likud party, leading to a virtual closing of the window of opportunity opened at Oslo.

In his treatment of such historically significant events, Rotenstreich would, in all probability, have followed his traditional way of dealing with these issues on a theoretical level, beyond daily politics and polemics. But being the kind of public philosopher he always was, he would not shy away from what these events, and especially the traumatic dimension of an assassination of a prime minister of the Jewish state by a Jewish fanatic, would mean to a theoretical assessment of Zionism. Without trying to second guess his response, one could however safely say that in many respects he would have felt vindicated, albeit sometimes in a tragic way.

For Rotenstreich's argument in this volume, as well as in his previous studies and essays on Jewish thought and Zionism, always viewed the renewal of Jewish political life in Israel as a consequence of an immanent tension between Jewish life in the Diaspora and the content of the Judaic tradition—but also as an unprecedented and revolutionary challenge to normative Judaism in its various forms. For all of its accommodationism to exilic existence, normative Judaism could not overlook the terrestrial dimension of the meaning of Jerusalem in the Jewish order of things; paradoxically, the more normative Judaism developed and flourished in exile, the more the contradictions of this diasporic existence became poignant. As Rotenstreich pointed out, in the two most accommodative phases of Jewish life in exile—medieval Muslim Spain and ninteenth-century Germany, the dream or the specter—of the Land of Israel would come back to haunt the thinking of Jewish philosophers, poets, and rabbinical writers, from Yehuda Halevi to Moses Mendelssohn to Franz Rosenzweig. It was also this issue that was responsible for some of the most acrimonious debates around the most thorough-going attempt to confront modernity—the Reform Movement in nineteenth-century Central Europe, mainly in Germany and Hungary (and later, of course, in the United States).

But Rotenstreich also realized how radical a break with normative Judaism and its development over two millennia of exile and powerlessness Zionism really was. Normative Judaism had no clear answers to the questions of power, its uses and abuses, since in exile Jews did not possess and wield it, and thus rabbinical thought could develop a quiet and neutral attitude toward it. This was epitomized in the Aramaic saying "dina de-malchuta dina," which can be loosely but accurately translated as "obey the law of the land." Such neutrality would be possible precisely because the law of the land was not formulated by a Jewish power and hence did not reflect any Jewish norms nor could it be measured by them. On another level, Rotenstreich argued repeatedly against infusing the State of Israel, living in the here and now with unattainable messianic aims. The consequences of such messianic expectations could be deadly.

The whole vexing complex of issues commonly called in the contemporary discourse, "state and religion in Israel," grew out of the radically innovative and unprecedented appearance of a Jewish polity, of Jewish public sphere—and hence of power. This occurred in a context of a modern Jewish nation-state where "Jewishness" could not be identical with Jewish religion as such for numerous reasons: Jewish religious precepts were developed under conditions of powerlessness, the core of the Zionist movement was not observant in the traditional Judaic sense, and, last and not least, the Jewish state numbered among its citizens many who were not Jewish. If one adds to this the contingent fact that Israel, from its inception, found itself in an existential struggle for survival, that is, in a constant state of war and emergency, one could really assess the depth of the poverty of normative Judaism in providing an arsenal of answers to the novel questions faced by a Jewish polity under such circumstances.

Although Rotenstreich was aware of the pitfalls presented by numerous cases of the abuses of political power by religious authorities in the modern Jewish nation-state, he was equally aware that the secular powers of nation-state unencumbered by ethical norms can be corrosive. In this he followed many of the strictures raised by Ahad Ha'am in his critique of purely political Zionism, and like him was looking for a modern, nonreligious construction of a Judaic tradition that could become a normative compass to a Jewish polity. The complexities of Rotenstreich's relationship to David Ben-Gurion, which led from an albeit critical yet basically positive evaluation to a radical break and public confrontation during the so-called Lavon Affair, suggest the multilayered potentialities of this approach.

Rotenstreich's numerous interventions in the political debate in Israel, which led him to contribute over the years hundreds of articles to the daily Hebrew press—a feat unusual for a philosopher of his stature—dealt mostly with these questions of morality and politics, where he saw that conventional Zionist thinking, being constantly buffeted by political and existential threats, suffered from a major deficit. For Rotenstreich, in a country like Israel, constantly in danger and intermittently but continuously at war, the ethical dilemmas were even more exacerbated, and in this sense his voice was in the prophetic tradition of speaking truth to power, going against the grain not only of the powers-that-be but also of an unbridled *vox populi.* In a democratic context, speaking truth to power meant for Rotenstreich also being ready to confront popular nostrums, sometimes widely accepted and universally held. Occasionally it took a lot of courage to stand up against such popular and populist opinions.

It was these considerations that were also responsible for Rotenstreich's moderate, human socialism. In socialist Zionism he saw, like A. D. Gordon in the early decades of the twentieth century, the preservation of some of the communitarian traditions inherent in the Jewish ethos. A philosophical critic of Marxism, especially in its Leninist version, Rotenstreich viewed the Soviet system as a major threat to humanist values and freedom. Yet notwithstanding this critique—which again he published, especially in the 1950s in numerous popular articles, when a part of the Zionist Left were still beholden to Stalinism—Rotenstreich viewed an unchecked capitalism as not conducive to a universal development of human values, and in the Zionist context as not being able to give an answer to a project that required high degrees of solidarity, sometimes under conditions of great personal sacrifice. For this reason, Rotenstreich was a mentor to many in the kibbutz movement. Zionists, in Rotenstreich's views, were their brothers' keepers, and an individualistic ethos could not supply the moral underpinning of a national project, which called for an ethics of responsibility and did not aim merely at individual fulfillment and achievement.

The massive immigration of Soviet Jews to Israel in the late 1980s and early 1990s, whose first waves Rotenstreich was able to witness, made him feel vindicated that the solidarity inherent in the Zionist ethos was still relevant and evident at hand and would continue to make demands on the Jewish people in general and of Israel and its social policies and arrangements in particular.

Similarly, Rotenstreich also argued the Israel–Diaspora relations should transcend their merely instrumental character. It would not suffice—neither for Israel nor for Diaspora Jews—if this relationship would be merely subsumed under the rubric of fund-raising and political lobbying. What was needed was a mutually enriching dialogue, where the different life experiences of the Jewish polity on the one hand and of a materially and intellectually rich Diaspora could be seen as complementary elements of a multifaceted Jewish life. Equally, however, Rotenstreich never subscribed to the neo-Babylonian construction of the Diaspora, especially of American Jewry, as being on an equal normative footing to that of Israel. Living in Israel and living in the Diaspora always remained for Rotenstreich as having different places in a normative Jewish hierarchy, and while a simplistic "negation of the galut" never appealed to him, he always argued about the immanent difference between them, which sometimes put an extra burden on Israeli Jews (like having to develop an ethics of power, a dilemma from which Diaspora Jews were instrinsically spared).

Nathan Rotenstreich was a public philosopher in the Platonic and Aristotelian tradition. At home in various philosophical traditions—from Kantianism to phenomenology and the philosophy of language—his was not the ivory tower's philosophy, but that of the *agora*—or in Hebrew-Aramaic, *parhessia*: the public arena. This volume is a testimony to his abiding power as philosopher and public thinker.

Nathan Rotenstreich on Issues Relating to the Holocaust

Appendix

The impact of the Holocaust on Jewish history at large and on Zionism in particular has been a subject of great interest. Nathan Rotenstreich discussed this issue in a postscript to the volume: *The Holocaust as Historical Experience,* which he edited with Professor Yehuda Bauer (Holmes & Meier, 1981):

> "I will refer to the changes that occurred in Jewish history, changes that were elicited by the Holocaust. It was pointed out that Jewish behavior then was by no means uniformly passive; even if the majority tended to seek adjustment, there were many islands of Jewish activity in spite of the total compulsion. What has happened since is that activity, initiative, or attempt to create our own realm, all this have become leading factors of Jewish life and Jewish experience, not islands of Jewish response in a sea of overwhelming compulsion. There was, of course, previously a continuous effort in Jewish history for the last eighty or a hundred years to give continuous expression to Jewish initiative. But the Holocaust greatly reinforced the impulse towards initiative. We now exhibit a readiness, willingness, even a compulsion to be active . . . And there is a new phenomenon of Jewish stubbornness. This is stubbornness in maintaining the Jews as an entity in the historical present . . ."

"The continuous effort" to which Rotenstreich refers in the above paragraph is of course the Zionist ideas and Movement. Zionism's objective was to return the Jews to the main course of history. The establishment of the Jewish State three years after the Holocaust was at the same time the utmost achievement for Zionism and reaction to the destruction of the Jews during WW II.

Adhering to Rotenstreich's view on this subject, we offer as an addendum to the main part of this volume two articles dealing with issues relating to the Holocaust.

The first one refers to the Eichmann Trial, which took place in Jerusalem in 1961. The second relates to the "Debate of the German Historians" (Historikerstreit), which occurred in the 1980s and was a major topic at that time. German historians and philosophers were debating the question of Nazism and whether it was unique in history, or part of a chain of events that happened during the first half of the twentieth century.

As a Kantian scholar Rotenstreich examined moral questions in many of his articles and books. In the essay relating to the Eichmann trial, he deals with arguments raised by Eichmann in his defense and broadens these discussions to the moral responsibility of every human being, adding historical and philosophical context to these issues. In the essay relating to the "Debate of the German Historians," and to Ernst Nolte's arguments in this debate in particular, Rotenstreich deals with historiosophical topics, focusing on the Holocaust and its uniqueness in history.

Ephrat Balberg-Rotenstreich

The Individual and Personal Responsibility

I

The question of the personal responsibility of a certain individual, says John Doe, concerning acts that were done by a group of individuals, a society, a people, or a state—necessarily arose in and around the proceedings of the Eichmann Trial. It arose in circles of those who are interested in such questions, and in circles of political and moral thinkers, who wish to establish principles concerning the behavior of the individual and his position.

As regards those who would lessen the responsibility cast on an individual for acts in which he participated, there are two opinions between which we must differentiate: (a) The first one being that acts of an individual, performed as a part of an organized state (as the Nazi regime was organized); or the acts of an individual who is carried away on a wave of general irrationality (ideological and psychological), such as marked the atmosphere and the so-called worldview (*Weltanschauung)* of the Nazi movement; or an individual involved in a cruel war, who is necessarily attached to one of the warring camps, and the side to which he is attached has iron discipline and customs—there is no way of holding such an individual personally and humanly responsible, and thus there certainly can be no legal responsibility. This is one thesis that we must be concerned with, and we must evaluate its weight, both intellectual and human.

This paper was first published in *Yad Vashem Studies*, vol. 5, 1963. Reprinted here with permission of the publisher.

(b) There is a second opinion, which was brought out during the proceedings of the Trial itself, in an exchange between a prosecution witness Professor Salo Baron, and the accused's attorney, Dr. R. Servatius. The intention of this opinion is different from that of the one previously mentioned. It also states, like the first thesis, that the individual is carried away by factors, commonly called "historical factors" beyond his control, such as, relations of the generation, traditions, climates of opinion, and so on. Thus the acts of man, whose behavior is determined by these factors, sometimes have results that are outside his declared intentions. Just as a man has no control over the factors that guide his acts and determine his behavior, thus he has no control over the results of the acts he performs, so sometimes the results in the future stands in blatant contradiction to the content and intention of the forces that determine his behavior in the present. As the defense counsel said: "Look, they wanted to destroy and to exterminate the people of Israel, but the scheme of the plotters was frustrated; a flowering state arose instead of this plot succeeding."[1] In stating this fact there is a certain attempt to lessen the guilt, and also the responsibility of the doer—for certainly there is room, and rightly so, to argue that a deed is judged not only by the intentions of the doer, but also by its results; even when there is a contradiction between the intentions and the results. According to the first thesis, one cannot hold a man responsible because of his place in the historical process of the past, while according to the second thesis, one cannot hold him responsible—or at least there is a diminution of responsibility—because of the historical process from present to future.

During the courtroom proceedings, a reliance upon the Historical School of Law (*Rechtsschule*) slipped in, in support of this thesis. We should set aside some space to the clarification of the connections between the ideas that were presented here, not to put this matter in its correct historical and factual order context, but to clarify the fundamental question before us. Seeing the moral meaning of the problem before us depends on this clarification.

II

At the heart of the Historical School's discussion of Law is the view that Law is not created by a directed and executed act of man, but is shaped in the historical process of the generations by internal powers, operating unostentatiously, as Savigny said. The human existence of each individual is, according to the view, linked to a whole, higher than himself: the wholeness of a family, a people or a state. Every period in the existence of a people is the continuation and development of prior periods.[2] This whole is not an external amalgam of the factors that compose it, but it has a power that affects and directs—the force that this school calls the "spirit of the people" (*Volksgeist*). Law, like any characteristic of a particular people, grows out of the common conviction (*Überzeugung*) of a people. This conviction is like those same internal, unostentatious forces that advance and reveal themselves in the changing generations.

But the School of Historic Law did not believe that there is a rational process in History and a process common to all peoples in which common human goals are materialized, and which can be expressed as principles of Reason. This has been assumed by those who envisaged that there is a common historical process of humanity that causes one continuous, progressive crystallization of freedom, or of the consciousness of freedom, or of the liberty and independence of people, or of equality between people. Thus, for example, thought Condorcet, on one hand, when he spoke of equality between people, and Hegel, on the other hand, when he spoke of a progressive consciousness of freedom, which characterizes the developing process of History. The Historical School spoke about the ties of man; the ties of personal existence as a link in a whole. But it is not at all clear whether from this follows the conclusion that the individual has neither initiative nor personal responsibility. This school spoke of the growth of Law and Language, of customs and mores, from the internal forces working unostentatiously. But it is not at all clear whether it follows that individual-private existence has no modes of behavior in it stemming from within itself and from itself alone; or whether we must say that it follows from the ideas of the Historical School that it is possible that a man should, in fact, by his acts, aim at one goal and actually achieve another, and that the goal achieved in spite of the doer, be more rational and justified than the goal the doer actually aimed at when he acted. There is no place for this idea in the Historical School; it is, however, a slight echo of one of Hegel's ideas. We will clarify this matter since just on it the correct distinction concerning the question of personal responsibility depends.

III

Hegel also talks of the "spirit of the people" (*Volksgeist*), but we will easily be able to see the difference between the concept as it is used in his doctrine, and in the Historical School of Law. He also says that the "spirit of the people" expresses itself in religion, worship, mores, customs, art, constitutions, and political laws. Hegel, however, believes that the "spirit of the people" is actually a moral spirit, and in his theory of the psychological or spiritual foundation of the state, he calls it "the divine foundation" that knows itself and desires itself.[3] This matter is of crucial importance, because from it we understand that the "spirit of the people" is a certain, partial materialization of the "spirit of the world," or of History in its generality. It exists as a partial embodiment and, by virtue of this, the history of a certain people, which is activated and effected by its spirit, is attached to the historic process of all mankind. Because the history of one people is placed within the general process, it is possible to think that the acts that occur within the confines of one people, and the relations between people will be looked at not only from the viewpoint of a local event within one community, but from the point of view of general, historical events. Only within the bounds of this conception is it possible to evaluate the results of the acts of an individual, or a people in relation to History in its entirety.

This bring us to the consideration, albeit abridged, of the ides of "the cunning of Reason" (*die List der Vernunft*), that Hegel formulated in his treatment of History. The man, says Hegel, who creates something worthy, puts all his energy into this effort; he hasn't the sobriety to want this thing or another thing; he doesn't disseminate himself and give his energy to these goals or others, but completely devoted to his great and true goal. Passion (*Leidenschaft*) is the force of this goal, and the determination of this is a certain type of urge, almost an animal urge, which is revealed when man puts his energy into the goal, which he wants to achieve. This passion is what is called "awakening," or "enthusiasm." Indeed, this passion is the drive of the active man, but, in truth, it is the pinnacle of a great idea. In fact this idea remains deep in the background and, apparently, doesn't take part in the actual process of events, nor in the contention about them. It sends the urge, or passion of the active man, out to work for it. The idea that uses drives, desires, and passions, acts with cunning as regards these desires; it uses them for its own ends in spite of the fact that these passions and desires have ends of their own. Reason's use of these drives is what Hegel calls "the cunning of Reason," and the historical example of this is: Julius Ceasar had to do what was necessary; he had to dispense with the blemished and tainted freedom of Rome. He himself fell in this struggle, but the necessary basis remained: Freedom lay beneath the external events. Individuals are considered here—and Julius Ceasar is the individual about whom we are talking, as an individual who proves the rule—from the point of view of being a means for the benefit of the realization of the great historical process; for example, for the benefit of the realization of the idea of Freedom. And from this point of view the historical individual is considered; whether or not he furthered the great historical process and the idea that this process is destined to materialize. When the historical individual is a means, it is possible to use him *via* cunning; that is, Reason puts him to work, by means of her cunning, in order to realize, through his partial and impulsive aims, her own fulfillment.[4]

A slight echo, as we said, of this idea was presented in the defense attorney's case, even though he relegated it to a different place, the place of the Historical School of the theory of Law. He wanted to say, that it was as if Reason used the extermination of the Jews in order to realize the freedom and independence of the Jews, against the will of those who sought to exterminate them.

The echo is certainly slight, because the whole discussion lacks the basic idea, from within which grew Hegel's worldview; that is to say, that there is a universal historical process, whose task is to materialize the idea of Reason, which is Freedom, or Consciousness of Freedom. But it is precisely because this echo is heard that we must ask ourselves: does it follow from this point of view that a man is freed from his own responsibility because his acts produced good results against his will? In order to answer this question we must perform two studies: one, the study of an idea and the other, the study of a text. From the standpoint of the idea, the question arises as to whether from the concept of the "cunning of Reason" follows the viewpoint that patent evil, declared and blantant evil, produces good results. In the historical examples that Hegel himself presents (like the example of Julius Ceasar, or that of Napoleon), the passions and drives of the active historical man, and his partial goals—such as desire for power—are always spoken of, and the man is driven toward their attainment. It can be said that Hegel brought out the irrational powers of an urge that serve rational goals, such as the drive for power that serves the goal of Freedom; or partial goals that serve as universal, such as France's domination of the European continent that served another goal—the freeing of these nations and the rise of consciousness of their nationality and their political and cultural freedom. But, in the text, we could not find him saying that a goal that he negates from a moral standpoint (such as the extermination of men for the sake of extermination, or removing human beings from the sphere of humanity—as if they were material, and turning them into material), can serve a great historical goal. There was no idea of the history of humanity in Nazi ideology, but there was an idea of the rule of the German people or a German reign over the world; and so one must not judge it according to an historical and conceptual outlook, wherein the process of events is specifically discussed from the point of view of world history, or a universal history of mankind. And, second, the acts that were performed were acts of monstrous and organized slaughter, that brought into action the mechanism of the state and the most highly developed technology in the world, for the cold-blooded extermination of huge numbers of people, simply because they were members of a particular group. These are acts that cannot be viewed as brought about by passion or partial intentions, but these are acts that must be judged from the standpoint of their place and from the standpoint of their nature, and the character of those who did them. And if we should use the concrete example mentioned—the rise of the Jewish State after the devastating slaughter of the Jews—when stripped to its essentials, this rise of a Jewish State is not a result of the Holocaust, even though it did create a certain climate of guilt among the people of the world, that paved the way for their readiness to atone for the guilt. Because the Holocaust erased from the Jewish people those Jewish groups who had sought, by themselves, to come to Israel, who brought forth the idea and the movement that bore the Jewish State, and who, because of the Extermination, were unable to come to the place they had sought. Every such slaughter, like murder, does not only annihilate that which is, but also the potential within it. The Nazi ideology, and the deeds caused by this ideology, had no such basis of respect for the human potential embodied in every man and also embodied in a Jew as a man. Never in the history of mankind has there been such an occurrence, wherein war was waged against human beings as if they were mere clay. The Jews were not merely considered an inferior race, but they were considered to be creatures outside the realm of humanity—and there is no basis for comparing this instance to other historical incidents of conflicts and struggles between peoples *and even struggles to the bitter end.* In another aspect of his philosophy, which we do not wish to study in detail here, Hegel argued that precisely in war, one people recognizes the other that is fighting, and admits its character as a people.[5] The war of the German people and state against the Jewish people was not built on recognition or acknowledgment of the Jewish people but on casting them out of the human realm; that same realm in which there is any possibility and sense to talk about reciprocal recognition and acknowledgment.

And as for the textual side, the same text in whose context the idea of the "cunning of Reason" is found, Hegel says that individuals are an end in themselves from the standpoint of the content of the idea of an end. Man is an end in himself by virtue of the divine factor hidden in him. So he says in the language of religion, known to us from the idea of "the image of God." Man is an end from the standpoint of his determining himself, from the standpoint of his being active, and from the standpoint of Freedom, to which he is tied. And to this aspect, he adds, is connected the phenomenon of guilt; as the mark of Man is that he knows what is good and what is bad, and is capable, by the power of his will, to choose either good or bad. In a word: that it is possible for him to be guilty. Only an animal is a guiltless creature. Guilt means the possibility of imputing to a man the acts that he performs (*Imputabilität*). It is no excuse, says Hegel, if it is said that Man is made by nature and circumstances. His liberty lies in the fact that his guilt is found in what he has done.

The basic question that stands before us now is: even when a man performs acts whose historical results encourage the materialization of a good goal, the acting man does not cease to be responsible for his present acts. And with this question we move away from the consideration of this relation, or any other, to the world of nineteenth-century German thought, and stand before the very question: should we view man as determined by the process of events, by History, or not? Is it only the heroic man who does not succumb to determination by historical processes and political events? If only the heroic man is liable to withstand this pressure then we cannot require a thing from just any individual. Just as we cannot order love, so we cannot give orders for heroism. Or should we assume that there is a plain basis, and not heroic elevation, underlying the role and the authority of the moral claim, which is determined by the views of an individual—anybody—and his concrete actions in the universe-in-itself? This is the question we now face. The clarification of this question can be detached from the proceedings of the Trial and the argument heard therein. The Trial merely serves as an opportune stepping-stone from which to clarify the question in its substance.

IV

The above-mentioned Historical School stressed the idea of internal acting forces, that determine the course of events within a domain, such as the legal system of a state, mores, worship, and so on. When we consider this idea, we must begin by realizing that it is not only an analysis of the active factors, and perhaps not at all an analysis of this kind, and not even a description of these causes. It is rather an ideology; it is to determine what *ought* to be the factors that act in shaping various areas of activity, and to demand from Man, or from a generation, or from statesmen, or from legislators, not to see themselves as authorities for passing laws, to ordain, to intervene, but to listen to what exists within the concealed treasure of the "soul" of the generations. Surely this School cannot propose this ideology, formulated in a demand, without both supposing the actual existence of these forces, and the possibility of listening and of unequivocally deciphering the inheritance of the generations; that is to say, that the voice of the generations is a one and only voice. From this standpoint, the idea of the "spirit of the people" rejoins, for all that it is expressed in ideological language, some discussions that suggest that national character exists.

Not national character as mere fact, but national character as the supreme instance, and as a directive authority. National character as fact becomes a directive authority by being presented as the "spirit of the people." It is well known how problematical this assertion is, because "national character" is expressed in institutions, and how close the possibility is that certain features of human beings affect the institutions, and that the institutions affect the people."

At any rate, we can here draw away from a scholastic discussion and return to the essential question: should we assume that Man is entirely determined by historical, psychological, social and other factors, and does not stand as an individual? Even if we say that Man is but a link in various wholes, we still have not said that there is no difference between his being a link in the wholeness of a family, and his being a link in the totality of a state. As if this meant that there were a preconceived harmony, or even a factual harmony between, for example, the orbit of the family, and the orbit of the nation. If the state demands that the father of a family give his son to arms, this does not mean that, as a father, he does not feel the pain of his son's going, nor, all the more so, the death of his son. Neither does the act cease to be a sacrifice, even if the state is victorious through the sacrifice of his son. Loss of life does not cease to be loss of life, even if it comes about for the benefit of the state, or the nation; or even if it advances the state and the people. This is the contradiction between the father's feelings—and even when he overcomes his feelings it still exists—and his acquiescence to the order of the state. However, a man is neither entirely in conflict nor is he determined completely by his being a part of one whole. The more links there are, the more contradiction are possible that the man will feel different feelings at the same time; the feelings of a father and the feelings of a citizen of his native land. There is thus no necessity to suppose any total determination that will cause all the feelings to be cut according to the same measure and the same type—that a man, as a father, should feel the same sensation that he feels as a son of his homeland.

And here we must add that no whole to which a man is attached can erase his entire internal world from his heart. The state can order him to behave in a certain way, but it cannot create in his heart a feeling about this particular behavior. It can order him to prefer her call to the call of being a father, but it cannot remove from his heart the feeling he has as a father. But the man himself can erase this feeling from his heart and give himself over entirely to the service of one whole. There is no reality that rules in any and all events, over every segment of the life of Man. Even the reality of political totalitarianism doesn't; without the acquiescence of the man to the reality, and without the meaning that he himself gives it, and without the concession that he himself concedes—there would be no threat of one's being eradicated by reality, not even the most totalitarian. The totalitarian reality can order a man to confess publicly to crimes that he did not commit, and he can perform the ritual of the confession down to its minutest details. But he himself is not constrained by this to feel in his heart that he did indeed commit a crime of which he is innocent. Man is not only a part within a whole that is beyond him; he also lives within the whole that is himself, and that whole cannot be abolished except by himself.

The last remnant of Man's autonomy cannot be abolished except by autonomy itself: autonomy can be eradicated only by itself.

We do not intend, by these remarks, to negate revealed facts—and how overwhelming they are—that there is compulsion, terror, necessity; that one adapts oneself to reality in the name of life, and so on. We do not intend, by these remarks, to say that the one and only revelation of autonomy is war and heroic rebellion against the negation of autonomy. Were we to say these things at all, we would thereby tend to identify autonomy with heroism. However, let us even suppose a man committing acts of extermination under duress, having no companion with whom he could go forth and rebel. And let us further suppose that the regime is organized, so that revolt can grow only though an organization that is equal to the organization against which it is in revolt. In spite of all this, the intention of his heart he can maintain alone. The addition of a cry of joy that he shouts when he is forced to do something, the removal from his heart a feeling of guilt at the time of the act, the existence of a written, or unwritten, diary of the most personal nature—these he can retain for himself; a one and only proclamation at that one and only time, announcing that he is not pleased with what he himself is doing and that the right conduct would have been for him not to have done what he was forced to do—these are the last remnants of the independence of a man, that cannot be crushed by the compelling force of the regime, but can be crushed by the individual himself. The last remnant of humanity—even when humanity lacks vigor and expression in acts—should not be surrendered; it is the last criterion of behavior within the human limits. It is mistaken to say that nonhuman behavior is bestial—one cannot demand a last remnant of autonomy from an animal; only from the autonomous is it possible to demand autonomy; he who does not fulfill it does not behave like an animal, but rather as one who uses his human powers in order to place himself outside of humanity. His guilt lies in the fact that he used the human in him in order to remove it from his heart.

Certainly the Nazi regime emphasized this side of the behavior of people, in the most frightful and terrible manner.

But we all, at every moment, stand before this simple question: When we do something in a moment of distress, are we forced to say and to think—and this is the crucial point—that the destruction which we wrought in a distressed moment is good in itself and not only a necessity of this crisis? It will indeed not be censured, but that does not mean that it will spontaneously become good, worthy, desired, something to be striven for, etc. A lack of manifold drives and reactions, and the making of one single drive not only dominant but also causing it to be the only one in existence—this is a basic question in human situations, a question that the Nazi period emphasized and placed before us in the real world, as if it were a world seen through a magnifying glass and not a real world.

A certain breaking away from the general course of events, and even if the course of events is of the most sweeping kind; a certain self-judgment, and even if it is a value-judgment of acts that a man himself does, and for which he has an explanation—that he does them for lack of choice in order to preserve his life, or his family's lives; even the hypocrites who do things with a contented heart—which they do not—all these are preferable to the contentment of the abolishment of self-restraint, the annihilation of the remnant of withdrawal from man's individual and independent relation to the world that encompasses him. A crime against humanity has an objective definition: the extermination of peoples and their removal from the orbit of life. But this crime is complemented by the subjective aspect as well, and without this complement the crime in its objective aspect would not be able to come into existence. That is, the abolishment of the human in the doer, when this man devotes himself completely and totally to this occupation of his, the occupation of extermination.

From this standpoint, we must see the idea of reliance on determination by the generations, by the people, by the state, by a historical period, and other such ideas that are heard not only in defense of people (and defense—even by a professional—is a certain manifestation of humanity), but are echoes of the Nazi ideology. This ideology really sought, as a basic demand in regards to Man, that he be determined by processes, military power that rules all, and the methods of rule over men. He who concerns himself with the individual who uproots his humanity from within him and leaves no shred of it in him at the hour of action, and regards this human individual as if he were only dust, or an instance in a biological species is, unawaredly perhaps, using an idea that is a modification of Nazi ideology. Complete determination by race, for example, cannot be assumed, without assuming that there is no individual remnant, or at least an individual remnant that has any weight, in an action in the real world. Whatever remains of individuality is here, itself, only natural, such as the morphological configuration of the individual, facial features, physionomical features, etc. But this precisely was an assumption of Nazi ideology; through this assumption the Nazi ideology was able to demand from the individual not to have a standing of his own; that he immerse himself in the run of events and make a tool of himself and free himself, by and through this, from any possible personal responsibility. When a man does not exist, there can be no personal responsibility. But when a man exists, and exists by his very nature in such a manner that he is not entirely determined by any state of affairs whatsoever, and not even by all the factors together—if he ceases to be a human being he does so from within himself and his responsibility lies in that he ceased to be a human being.

He who argues that he is not responsible for his acts because he was caught within a system over which he had no control—either argues in fact, that he is not an active human being, or that he was not an active human being before. But if a man acts through decision or by setting individual goals for himself and participating in setting the goals of the public sphere to which he belongs; if he reacts to what happens in the world by analyzing—seeing the causes and the effects, and weighs the force of the different factors in reality; if he knows, and is conscious of the nature of the system and accepts the yoke of hierarchy and behaves in accordance with what it implies—he didn't uproot the mechanism of human action from himself; he didn't completely surrender his capacity of analysis. He only argues that it is only in relation to responsibility for his acts that he did not act as a man, but as one immersed in circumstances, as if he himself were a circumstance. Surely there is in this a blatant contradiction; not a logical contradiction but a concrete one. A person cannot both maintain the power of resonance of his consciousness in relation to the understanding of reality and not maintain it, at the very same time, in relation to the evaluation of reality and evaluation of himself and his acts in reality. Distinction and evaluation—both are revelations of the same distinguishing consciousness of men. When one aspect of consciousness in active, that which distinguishes the area of perceiving reality as a state of affairs, the second aspect, in the area of the evaluation of reality, also is active. Moreover, evaluating reality from the standpoint of the meaning of the acts done, insofar as they harm Man and Humanity, and seeing the fact of the extermination of people as a primordial and basic evil, requires none of those exceptional powers of distinction and analysis, needed sometimes for the factual and descriptive understanding of reality. In this way moral judgment is more elementary, since it revolves around a matter revealed in its meaning—such as the lives of human beings. It is more elementary than theoretical judgment, understanding, knowledge, and familiarity with the process and other matters of importance when we wish to know the reality in which we act or the environing state of affairs.

V

There is, however, an essential relation of mutual dependence and mutual determination between the humanity in me and that in my fellow man. Since Man himself is composed of different levels, which include the level of his own personal world, be it weak, limited, and enclosed in itself, when he stands before his fellow man, he cannot but recognize that the man before him is made up of many levels too; that his fellow man is also a human being and has humanity in him, since he is made up of many levels. Why does a man not activate his humanity in relation to the extermination that he sees, but, rather, helps it to materialize? It seems that the answer is as follows: he does not recognize that in the act of extermination the humanity of he who is exterminated is violated, since in the eyes of the exterminator he who is exterminated is not a human being; the exterminated are, in no way, a group of people. The humanity of a man is activated when he thinks about what is done, and his thoughts cause him to consider the one who is affected by the act. But if his consideration is hidden from himself then surely it will not show in his acts. Without a worldview that negates the humanity of human beings there can be no extermination of these people as the Nazis organized it—through their state and its system. However, because there is such a worldview that argues that people exist who are not human beings but material, the humanity in Man is not aroused, since there is no occasion for it to be aroused; and certainly it was aroused among those who viewed the exterminated as people, and it was not aroused among those who did not see them in this light.

Here we see to what extent, all in all, this descriptive, and apparently distinguishing worldview—that differentiates by virtue of a number of qualities and characteristics, between those who are within the realm of man, and those who seem biologically to be human beings, but in fact are not—had practical consequences. Moral behavior, or rather immoral behavior, in truth, was rooted in an outlook about facts that can arise because of a loss of humanity in the doer. But the worldview itself, that there are people who are not human beings, the fact of attributing humanity to some people, and denying this humanity to others—is basically immoral. Vis-à-vis this view, there is no way of acting with tolerance, as we do and ought to do with the worldviews of people—even when we think that they are mistaken—because these are the views of human beings. We have esteem for the bearer of the worldviews and by virtue of our esteem we also come to esteem the worldviews themselves. But he who holds the view that there are people who are not human beings, cannot and may not demand esteem and consideration from us, because his view negates the very basis on which it and its creations stand; that is to say, that the worldview is produced by a man as human being, and that every man has a "view" of the world and of himself, be it dim, or undeveloped, or mistaken. The sin is not only in the extermination, but also in the worldview that was held, because the extermination then could be considered as being beyond evil, since it does not affect human beings at all.

We behave justly, by and large, according to the rule that one doesn't punish worldviews, but deeds. We agree to this rule, and we hold a man responsible, if, because of him, reality will be different than it was previously; if he had let reality remain as it had been, then he would not have been called to order. Responsibility is connected to a change that the doer brings to the process of events; and a view is generally considered as not causing a change in reality. This is generally correct, but it seems as if this were not true regarding the matter before us. The mere fact of denying the humanity of people as individuals, and of people as a group—this very worldview seemingly does not cause a change in apparent reality but does cause a change, which may be called metaphysical—and for which it is brought to face justice and held responsible as a worldview; since this worldview brings about acts and historical processes that are horrible in their dimensions, and devastating in their manifestations.

These remarks were made because of the necessity of clarifying the basic problems in question, which have nothing in common with judicial problems in the sense defined and peculiar to this concept. Insofar as we are involved with the matter of a trial and a court, this is only for the needs of a basis of clarification and not for the purpose of drawing conclusions on the level of the Trial. But certainly a trial is not removed from the roots of morality: on the contrary; it is one of the attempts that men make in order to realize morality through the trial, and the logic of its realm. Placing personal responsibility, and not punishment, is the principal.

Notes

1. *The Attorney-General versus Adolf Eichmann,* proceedings of the 13th session, 5th of Iyyar (April 24, 1961).

2. See Friedrich Karl Savigny, *Vom Beruf unserer Zeit für Gestzgegung und Rechtswissenschaft,* 1814.

3. Georg Wilhelm Friedrich Hegel, *Die Vernunft in der Geschichte,* Hamburg: 1955, p. 59 ff. Cf. S. Brie, *Der Volksgeist bei Hegel und in der historischen Rechtsschule*, Berlin and Leipzig, 1909.

Jewish thought in the nineteenth century was involved with and helped by this concept of the "spirit of the people." See my book: *Jewish Thought in Modern Times,* vol. 1 (in Hebrew), Tel Aviv: 1945, p. 222 ff. There one will also find references on this subject.

4. Hegel, *op. cit.,* p. 105 ff.

5. Georg Wilhelm Friedrich Hegel, *Die absolute Religion,* Leipzig: 1929, p. 104.

The Holocaust as a Unique Historical Event

> I have been a shadow
> Mine was another creator.
>
> —Dan Pagis[1]

The following remarks are related to the illuminating analysis presented by Professor Peter Pulzer in his article '*Erasing the past: German historians debate the Holocaust.*'[2]

Professor Pulzer is right to distinguish two approaches to the way the historical present relates to the historical past: that of Ranke who advocates accounting for the past from its own sources and its own perspective and that of Croce who emphasizes the involvement of the present in the past and of the past in the present. Croce's view, that all history is contemporary history, formally states that there are thematic relationships between the present and the past. Because of the mutual involvement of the two dimensions, when a researcher deals with the past from a perspective detached from his own situation, this becomes a significant act. Dealing with the past from within is even more significant precisely because of the past's bearing on the present. The dependence of the present course of events on the events of the past does not excuse the researcher from having to exercise sober judgment in all consciousness of the problems attendant on any contemporary study of past collective experience. Hegel's statement, that whatever we are, we are

---

This article was first published in: *Patterns of Prejudice*, vol. 22, no. 1, 1988. Reprinted here with permission of the publisher. http//www.tandf.co.uk

also historical (*geschichtlich*) creatures,[3] can be interpreted as pointing to the distinction between total involvement and the attempt to interpret with maximum detachment.

The Singularity of Historical Events

There is, however, another theoretical aspect of the German controversy, which did not receive attention although it is also related to the thematic relationship between the dimensions of time. Heinrich Rickert posed the question as to whether the conceptual distinction between asserting facts and formulating concepts[4] has any meaning in the study of history. The question is a relevant one for the natural sciences as well, once we are aware of the interrelation and even dependence between the assertion of facts or events and the theoretical or hypothetical scientific framework. The existence of atoms or electrons, for example, cannot be confirmed without the framework of a theory of particles, let alone an overarching theory of the functional relationships between events. But one difference between the two disciplines that does emerge is that the historical context is a comprehensive sphere and the individual events parts of the whole, whereas in the science of nature, individual phenomena are examples of the general theory.[5] One can conclude that history, that is historical science or research, can attempt to present reality, but not with regard to the general, only with regard to the particular, because it is only the particular, which really takes place.[6] It therefore seems surprising that those German historians who deal with the Nazi past and the Holocaust in the context of the Gulag, seem to ignore the concept of the singularity of historical events. Recognition of such a concept would have forestalled the various attempts to question the uniqueness of the Holocaust. I shall now discuss the conceptual confusion surrounding that issue before commenting on the substance of the debate.

Auschwitz and the Gulag

The conceptual confusion manifested in Ernst Nolte's writings can be illustrated by several examples. He states that the Third Reich should not be studied in isolation even within the framework of the 'Epoch of Fascism.'[7] What does Nolte mean here by isolation? He goes on to say that the singularity of the Third Reich cannot be denied but that penetrating analysis shows it to be a part of the history of mankind.[8] This can strike the reader as a banal statement. Historical events, including the Nazi regime and its deeds, are part of a historical context, whether that context is seen diachronically or synchronically. To rule over the world presupposes the reality of the world, not only as a material globe but also as the sum total of events. The Nazi regime is, because of its historical character, part of historical reality. But a totalitarian regime is not the total given reality. It is created.

The attempt to overcome this pseudo-isolation becomes apparent when Nolte argues that: 'Auschwitz is not primarily a result of traditional anti-Semitism. It was in its core not merely a "genocide" but was above all a reaction born out of the anxiety of the annihilating occurrences of the Russian Revolution. This copy was far more irrational than the original . . . .'[9] Can the relationship between the original and the copy explain the relation between the broad scope of historical events and the particular path of events related to the Third Reich? What does Nolte mean by 'copy' and 'original' here? That the Nazi regime imitated the Russian atrocities? Then what is the meaning of imitation in this context? Is it like sitting opposite a painting and trying to draw something similar to it? The so-called annihilation of the Jews under the Third Reich, the argument goes, was a reaction to or a distorted copy of another event, not an initiating or an original act. But looking at historical events, at initiatives of governments and the bodies subordinated to them, any act, any implementation of an order or the giving of an order, even when parallels can be found, must be decided upon by human beings, who, because they are exercising a decision, cannot be seen as imitators only. It is their decision, their way of implementing what they have learned from the historical events that preceded them. In the Nazi case further questions arise: why was their decision to undertake annihilation applied to the Jews? If this policy was not a catastrophic continuation of traditional anti-Semitism and just a copy of the Gulag, why were the Jews singled out?

Nolte's Conceptual Confusion

Was it a copy? The annihilation of the Jews was grounded in the view that the Jews are worse than an inferior race: they are not human beings at all. This point of view, one that is specifically race-linked is original, not copied. The Soviet atrocities, which go by the common heading of Gulag, certainly occurred but were related to class struggles and therefore to specific historical circumstances. Theoretically, if this term can be applied here, these circumstances can undergo a change when people shift from one class to another, or from one line of support to another. But when human beings are defined by their biological descendence, a definition that implies not only a negative evaluation but also a negation of their humanity, they can not change this pre-determined position. And if they face a destructive regime bent on ruling the world and, as a precondition, erasing the existence of pseudo-human beings, they cannot save themselves. No historical deed, no individual act can change the predetermined situation.

This conceptual confusion has grave consequences, including ethical ones. Nolte only compounds the confusion when, in another paper, referring to mass murder and the Soviet situation, he speaks about the probable causal connection (*kausaler Nexus)* between the Nazi regime and the Soviet paradigm.[10] What is the meaning of causal connection in this context? Is the Gulag situation the cause and the Nazi regime and its acts an effect? Does this correlation replace that between the original and the copy or is it a reinterpretation of it? The existence of a causal connection postulates more than a sequence in time, it implies a direct dependence. In this case it implies that the Gulag situation brought about the Nazi regime and its behavior, as if this relationship is similar to that between unemployment and protest, inflation and the disruption of the economic system or the decision to use the gas chambers and the operation of these chambers. To employ in this context the notion of a causal connection means going beyond the broad scope of a historical situation to set up a linear connection between one set of events and another. Furthermore, when a series of events is presented as the effect of a specific cause, the presentation itself suggests an excuse. It is only the result, we say, the response to a stimulating factor or incentive. The metaphor of the 'original' and its 'copy' implied that a decision is being made against a background of consciousness. The cause-and-effect model dispenses with mediation, implying something automatic and reflexive. There is obviously a conceptual confusion here. And we cannot ignore the innuendoes of that confusion, namely the drive toward de-delegitimization of the Nazi regime, even when dressed in quasi-conceptual formulations.

Cause and Effect

On several occasions, Nolte refers to '[Chaim Weizmann's official declaration] in the first days of September 1939, according to which Jews in the whole world would fight on the side of England . . . [This] might,' he continues, 'justify the consequential thesis that Hitler was allowed to treat the German Jews as prisoners of war and by this means to intern them.'[11] What is the significance of the date September 1939? Does it not refer to the first days of the war launched by Hitler? Did Weizmann react to the declaration of the war and to the first steps of it *ex nihilo*? Did not the Hitler regime have a 'Jewish policy' from the beginning of its tenure? Was not the negation of the Jews in the sense discussed before part and parcel of the Nazi program? Let us suppose for one moment that Jews did identify themselves with Weizmann's statement, and that Jews could, therefore, be considered prisoners of war. Questions remain. Are prisoners of war objects for annihilation and gas chambers? Were only German Jews prisoners of war and not Jews of Eastern Europe? By introducing Weizmann's comment into a discussion of the Holocaust Nolte once again reveals that his argument, far from being an analysis, is in fact a series of sporadic statements made by a lawyer pleading his case. This position taken by Weizmann is not explained in terms of a response or reaction to the regime and its policy. The implication that Weizmann's statement can be seen as the cause of Hitler's treatment of the Jews—the effect—is entirely inappropriate. Indeed, what comes to the fore is not the 'original' but the Nazi response to it.

The Race-Class Analogy

The conceptual confusion manifested in Nolte's use of the 'original' and 'copy' model also characterizes the argument which not only draws an analogy between the atrocities of the Nazi and Soviet regimes[12] but also an analogy between 'race' and 'class.' The latter analogy is one of the major points Joachim Fest makes in his article in the *Frankfurter Allgemeine Zeitung*.[13] He refers to a speech made in 1918 by the head of the Cheka secret police, Martyn Latsis, who stated that punishment and liquidation were no longer a question of guilt but of social belonging. What determines the 'destiny of the accused,' he went on, is to what class he belongs, where he comes from, what kind of education he has and what profession. According to this view, class cannot be 'chosen,' it 'sticks' to the person from birth throughout his life. Thus, the conclusion is that class, a socio-historical phenomenon, and race, a biological phenomenon transcending historical change, can be seen as parallel or analogous.

But even a Soviet statement cannot change the ontological difference between class and race. The historical character of class is part of its definition. Nothing can alter that core. Perhaps what was meant was to over-emphasize the power of class conditioning, as if those who are involved in the process were facing a natural phenomenon. This is not just conceptual confusion, it is also a deliberate tool to overpower the listener with words. What the Soviet spokesman did in terms of his quasi-conceptual frame of reference to those who present the pseudo-parallelism between class and race so deliberately, was to make them conscious of the conceptual confusion in the Soviet statement. Looking at these things from a broader perspective, with an awareness of what the concept of 'class' means, we know, for instance, that some of the 'founding fathers' of socialism and, hence, of communism, did not belong to the proletariat. Marx's biography is well-known. We are aware also of the distinction between 'interest in itself' and 'interest for itself,' the latter implying the awareness of those involved in the class struggle. Without that awareness there is no way to direct the historical process toward revolution. And that awareness is related to the class situation, but because to be aware is to be conscious, it is not determined by belonging to a certain class. These are only a few examples of the impossibility of transposing the inherent meaning of race on the concept of class and its position in the social struggle. Race is a biological phenomenon, though its interpretations in nineteenth-century theories and in the ideology of Nazism are attempts to attribute to race the power to determine the behavior and, as far as the Jews are concerned, their status as subhumans.

When the head of the Cheka overemphasized the position of class he did so not only through a lack of precision but also in order to emphasize that the terror and the atrocities caused by it could not be helped. Not only is this pseudo-conceptual pseudo-analysis, its introduction into the debate is meant to show that 'there is nothing new under the sun.' This is more than an attempt to present the Nazi situation as part of human history, which, as we said before, is a trivial statement, it is an attempt to show that there is nothing unique, in the broad sense of that term, about the Nazi situation. The arguments that the Nazis' actions were preconditioned or a copy of an original are meant to be of an apologetic character. If we overcome the singularity of the phenomenon and place it in the context of history and general patterns of behavior, the apology is not only emotional and sentimental, it takes on pretensions of being based on facts.

The Originality of the Nazis' Science of Murder

Is it accidental that in these discussions the notion of the science of murder, as analyzed by Benno Müller-Hill,[14] is not even mentioned? Müller-Hill's book deals mainly with the science of genetics and its appropriation by the Nazi regime and ideology. Is it an accident that this happened to the science of genetics—the science of determination by genes and thus of the position of biological descendence within the human context? This is not a matter of *Weltanschauung* as would be the case in the controversy between Lamarckian and Darwinian theories, or in the rejection of an attempt to question the validity of causality in physics. This is a direct subordination of a scientific discipline to a regime and its ideology. The science of genetics took upon itself to serve the ideology of race.

An attempt has been made to interpret one totalitarian regime, the Soviet one, as an original model for another totalitarian regime, the Nazi one. The Nazi regime, however, grounded itself in the totality of nature because it based itself on race as a phenomenon or pseudo-phenomenon of nature. Thus superiority and inferiority were determined by nature. But the totality of nature is not an attribute of a political regime. Totalitarian is an attribute, totality is a datum; the acceptance of the latter may be ideological but it is not created by an ideology.

To be sure, 'Auschwitz is not primarily a result of traditional anti-Semitism,'[15] Could Auschwitz be the result of any tradition? It is a result of the deliberate planning and execution of a policy. That policy integrated traditional anti-Semitism into the contemporary context and resulted in specific acts. The totalitarianism of the Nazi regime was not only related to its 'quasi-industrial manner,'[16] it was also an attempt to express the totality in totalitarianism as the sum total of the components of political, social, and ideological behavior. There is a strange similarity between Hannah Arendt's presentation of 'the banality of evil' and the *leitmotif* of the historical argument according to which the Nazi regime is a copy of an original, and thus cannot be seen as a unique phenomenon. The contextual and conceptual generalizations made are meant to justify the statement that 'all this constitutes singularity but it does not alter the fact that the so-called annihilation of the Jews during the Third Reich was a reaction or a distorted copy and not a first or original act.'[17] It is enough to point to the use of the description 'so-called annihilation' to make us realize what sort of argument this is. By emphasizing the aspect of reaction, which is meant to take away from the Nazi phenomenon its primary character and turn it into a response, the element of initiative is belittled if not eliminated.

In conclusion, it is appropriate to mention Kant's interpretation of the *Urbild* according to which copies are imperfect since they derive from the archetype only the material of their potential. They approximate to the prototype in varying degrees, 'yet always fall far short of actually attaining it.'[18] The question remains: in the relationship between the Bolshevik atrocities and the Nazi-initiated Holocaust where and what is the prototype and where and what the copy? The chronological sequence does not determine the answer. The quasi-imitation is the original.

Notes

1. Dan Pagis, the late poet and Hebrew University scholar, was himself a Holocaust survivor.

2. *Patterns of Prejudice*, vol. 21, no. 3. See also Gordon A. Craig, 'The war of the German historians,' *New York Review of Books*, 15 January 1987. The debate over singularity of the Holocaust is not related to the question of whether the Nazi initiative in launching the war against the Soviet Union can be interpreted as a 'preventive strike.' On this issue see Gerd, R. Ueberchair, "Historikerstreit" und "Präventivkriegsthese," in den Rechtfertigungs-versuchin des deutschen Überfall an die Sowjetunion 1941,' *Tribüne*, no. 103, 1987, 108. Jürgen Habermas's critical contributions to the debate on German historiography are now gathered in his *Ein Art Schadensabwicklung* (Frankfurt, 1987).

3. *Geschichte der Philosophie* (Leipzig, 1944), 1, 12.

4. Heinrich Rickert, *Die Grenzen der naturwisschenchaftlichen Begriffsbildung* (Tübingen und Leipzig, 1902), 314.

5. Ibid., 393.

6. Ibid., 251.

7. Ibid., 37.

8. Ernst Nolte, 'Between myth and revisionism? The Third Reich in the perspective of the 1980s' in W. Koch (ed.), *Aspects of the Third Reich* (London, 1985), 36.

9. Ibid.

10. Ernst Nolte, 'Vergangenheit, die nicht vdergehen will. Eine Rede, die geschrieben, aber nicht gehalten wereden konnte,' *Frankfurter Allgemeine Zeitung*, 6 June 1986. Also see Nolte, 'Die Sach auf den Kopf gestellt. Gegen den negativen Nationalismus in der Geschichtsbetrachtung,' *Die Zeit*, 31 October 1986.

11. Nolte, 'Between myth and revisionism,' 27–28.

12. Ibid., 35.

13. Joachim Fest, 'Die geschuldete Erinnerung. Zur Jkontroverse über die Unvergleichbarkeit der nationalsozialistischen Massenverbrechen,' *Frankfurter Allgemeine Zeitung*, 29 August 1986.

14. Benno Müller-Hill, *Tödliche Wissenschaft: Die Aussonderung von Juden, Zigeunern und Geisteskranken 1933-1945* (Hamburg 1984).

15. 'Between myth and revisionism,' 36.

16. Ibid.

17. Ibid.

18. *Kritik der reinen Vernunft* (Critique of Pure Reason) (trans. Kemp Smith) (New York/Toronto 1965), 492.

Index

Compiled by Michal Laks

A

Agriculture, 76, 77, 103
Ahad Ha'am, 1–45 passim, 5, 60, 76, 87–100 passim, 116, 117, 126, 129; and "negation of Galut," 92; and problem of Judaism, 117
America, United States of, 20, 23, 35, 37, and Jewish emancipation, 71; emigration of Jews to, 77, 118, 119, 123, 128
Anti-Semitism, 53, 59; emergence of term in C19th; 99, 119; in USA, 119, 157, 162
Arabs, 39, 41, 42, 59, 61, 62, 103, 124, 125, 126; conflict with Israel, nationalism of, 81
Arendt, Hannah, 162
Ariel, 72
Arlosoroff, Victor, *Der Judische Volkssocialismus*, 72
Assimilation, 1–45 passim, 99, 120
Athens, 112
Auschwitz, 156, 157, 162
Auto-emancipation, 59, 66, 68, 71; and creativity, 97

B

Baer, Yitzhak, 90; *Galut*, 98
Balfour Declaration, the (1917), 104
Bein, A., *Der neue Antisemitism and seine Bedeutung fur die Judenfrage*, 72
Ben Bezalel, Judah Lowe; *see* Maharal of Prague
Ben-Gurion, David, 1–45 passim, 129
Berdichevsky, Mikhah Joseph, 74, 85, 92, 93, 99; and renaissance, 74
Bergman, Shmuel Hugo, 10, 11
Bible, the, 20, 31, 32, 70, 71, 75, 76, 78, 80; and the Talmud, 82
Bohm, Adolf, *Die Zionistische Bewegung*, 60
Brenner, Joseph Chaim, 92, 93, 99
British, mandatory power, 103
Buber, Martin, *On Zion: The History of an Idea*, 60

C

Canaanism, 33
Captivity, 47
Civilization, 39, 40, 70, 77, 79, 80, 108, 109, 110, 111, 120; technological and urge to conquer and control nature, 108
Continuity, 37, 79, 80, 82, 83, 96, 97, 98, 104, 110; and Hebrew language, 80

Creativity, 10, 55, 70, 71, 73, ch. 3 passim, ch. 4 passim, 117, 119, 120; and survival, auto-emancipation, 97
Culture, 7, 19, 33, 38, 41, 56, 71, 73, 78, 79, 80, 90, 106; scientific, 87; modern, 94; universal, 10, 79, 94, 95, 120
Culture, Jewish, 78, 110; and continuity, 110
Croce, Benedetto, 155
Cheka, 160, 161
Christianity, 53, 63, 79; grounded in Judaism, 79

D

Defense, 105, 107; and character of Israeli society, 112
Democracy, 37; and Israeli society, 84
Diaspora, 1–45 passim, 69, 71, 76, 79, 81, 83, ch. 4 passim, 107, 110, 115, 116, 122, 131; exodus from as precondition for realization of full scope of commandments, 69; as exile, 22, 50; as punishment, 40, 88; impossibility of maintaining national Jewish existence within, 88
Dispersion, 1–45 passim, 49, 87, 88
Dreyfus Affair, significance for Herzl, 54
Dubnow, Shimon, and autonomy in the Diaspora, 92
Durkheim, Emile, *The Science of Normality*, 72

E

Economic growth, ch. 5 passim
Education, 23, 106; Jewish, in modern world, 97; minimal goal of, 97; Lessing's view of, 116
Eichmann, A., 137–154 passim
Eizenstadt, Stuart E., assimilation, 99
Emancipation, 1–45 passim, 49, 54, ch. 2 passim, 75, 97, 104, 112; and secular modernization of French Jewry, 63; through legislation, 84
Enlightenment, Jewish, 94
Europe, 1–45 passim, 54, 64, 71, 73, 75, 96, 104, 118, 120, 121, 128, 142, 159
Europe, Eastern and Central, 96, 118, 128; and anti-Semitism, 96
Exile, 1–45 passim, 50, 121, 128; as punishment, 88; as dispersion, 87
Exodus, and denial of Diaspora, 87, 93
Expatriation, 87

F

Fest, J., 160, 164
Frankel, J., *Socialism and Jewish Nationalism in Russia*, 72
Frankfurter Allgemeine Zeitung, 160, 163, 164
Fundamentalism, 48

G

Galut. *See* Diaspora, negation of
Germany, 52, 63, 128, 142, 143, 155–164
Ghetto, 67; as national disaster, 93
Giddens, Anthony, 72
God, 47, 50, 51
Gordon, Aharon David, 76, *Selected Essays*; 85; and "parasitic" occupations of Jews in the Diaspora, 90, 130
Gordonia Youth Movement, 1–45 passim
Gulag, 155–164 passim
Guttman, Julius, 2

H

Habermas, Jurgen, *The Philosophical Discourse of Modernity: Twelve Lectures,* 59, 72

Halakha, 83
Halevi, Yehuda, 128
Halperin, Ben, *The American Jew: A Zionist Analysis*, 99
Halutsiyut, Haluts, 1–45 passim
Hebrew, 38, 39; language of tradition, 64, 66; return to, 71; in State of Israel, 70; literature, 78
Hegel, Friedreich W., 3, 155–164 passim
Herzberg, Arthur, *Zionist Idea: A Historical Reader*, 60
Herzl, Theodor, 40, 57, 66, 67, 76, 91, 116, 125; analysis of hatred of the Jews, 54; *Der Judenstaat,* 59; significance of Dreyfus Affair for, 66
Hess, Moses, 52, 53, *Rome and Jerusalem,* 59, 65; and socialism, 65; and significance of Italian unification, 78
Hitler, Adolph, 159
Holmes, James S., and Hasns van Marle: *Men and Ideas*, 72
Holocaust, the, 18, 19, 21, 37, 104; changed profile of Jewish people, 77; as impetus for creation of the State of Israel, 143, 137–154 passim, 155–164 passim
Huizinga, Johann, 85; *Patriotism and Nationalism in European History,* 72
Human rights, 118
Hungary, 128

I

Ideology, 1–45 passim; national, Jewish, 56, 58; classical Zionist, 42, 88, 95, 116; Zionist, new formulation of, 98; Zionist, 88, ch. 6 passim; and morale, 101
Intifada, 126
Islam, and relation to Judaism, 63
Israel, army, ch. 5 passim; and *Tohar ha-Neshek,* 113–114
Israel, Land of, 24, 38–40, 55, 57, 60, 64, 69, 70, 75, 82, 87, 91, 124, 128; and territorial basis of Zionism, 64; return to as opposed to universalism, 69; interest in history of, 35; and return, 69, 73
Israel, State of, 1–45 passim, 59, 61, 69, 71, 75,, 80–85, chs. 4, 5, 6; and technological development, 70; and infrastructure of continuity, 80; and coexistence with the Diaspora, 59; focus of Jewish identification, 36
Italy, 59; unification of, 65; C17th Jewish thought in, 90

J

Jeremiah, 47, 50
Jerusalem, 128
Jewry, American, 123, 125, 126, 131, 1–45 passim
Jewry, European, 19, 21, 121; destruction of, 77, 78, 79, 104; conception of renaissance, 79; shift to USA, 118; and the Holocaust, 118; orthodox orientation of, pre-World War II, 118
Jewry, North African and Asian, 107
Jewry, South American, 118
Jewry, Soviet, 110, 118, 130
Jewry, Western, 19, 96, 98, 123; and goal of emancipation, 71
Jews, Diaspora, 22–24, 33, 41–43, 8, 130; shift from Europe of USA, 71; non-involvement in agriculture and industry, 76
Judaism, 3, 38, 39, 45, 48, 57, 63, 68–71, 79, 85, 93, 118, 120, 121; and secularity, emancipation, and the rule of law, 62; relationship with Christianity and Islam,

Judaism *(continued)*
53, 63; traditional, 95; and cultural cohesion, 116; Ahad Ha'am's analysis of, 38, 42, 116; normative Judaism, 128–129

K

Kant, Immanuel, 1–45 passim, *Religion within the Limits of Reason Alone,* 99, 163
Kantianism, 6, 131
Karaism, 33
Katz, Jacob, *Jewish Emancipation and Self Emancipation*, 60
Kaufman, Yehezkel, *Exile and Alienation,* 93
Kibbutz, 1–45 passim
Klal Israel, 1–45 passim
Knesset, 14, 26

L

Lavon Affair, 129
Lavon, Pinchas, 2
Leninism, 130
Lessing (G.E.), and the education of mankind, 116
Likud, the, 127
Lilienblum, M.J., 51
Luzzato, Simcha, 50, 51, 59

M

Maharal of Prague, 50, 59
Mamlakhtiyut, 16, 17, 18, 20, 45
Manual labor, 103
Mapai, 1–45 passim
Marr, W., 72
Marx Karl, 1–45 passim, 160
Marxism, 130
Mendelssohn, Moses, 128
Messiah, the, 57, 67, 68
Messianism, 19; and Zionism, 124
Middle Ages, 73, 90
Militarism, 113. *See also* war
Mixed marriages, and Jewish education, 97
Modernity, 1–45 passim, chs. 1, 2, 3 passim, 88, 90, 95, 96, 128; rejection of fundamentalism, 48; and the scientific method, 48; and secularism, 49; and the social contract, 49; and Jewish nationhood, 56; and basis of Zionism, 63
Morale, 15; of society, and ideology, 101
Muller-Hill, Benno, 161, 164

N

Nationalism, 38, 39, 58, 65, 72; Italian, 57; Jewish, Arab, and Palestinian, 59, 81, 125
Nature, 48, 62, 85, 88, 108, 162
Nazism, Nazi regime, 155–164 passim
Netanyahu, Binyamin, 127
Neumann, Emanuel, 25
Nolte, Ernst, 155–165 passim
Normalcy. *See* normality
Normality (also normalization), 33, 67, 72, 81; definitions of, 67; and adoption by Zionism, 67; and creating a structure of existence similar to other peoples, 76; and society, territory, and sovereignty manifested in statehood, 76; and renaissance, 77; and State of Israel, 80

O

Odessa, Jews in, 78
Oslo Accords, 127

P

Pagis, D., 155
Palestinians, 39; and Palestinian nationalism, 125; 129
Phenomenology, 131
Philosophy of language, 131
Pines, J.M., 51
Pinsker, J.L., 1–45 passim, 53, 59; views on clash between Jews and

the surrounding world, 53; *Auto-emancipation*, 59; and political Zionism, 76
Productivization, 55; and restructuring of Jewish professions, 103
Public realm, 82, 105, 122, 123
Pulzer, Peter, 155

R

Rabbinic courts, 85
Rabin, Yitzhak, 155
Race, 52, 137–154 passim, 155–164 passim
Ranke, Leopold von, 163
Rawidowicz, Simon, 27, 28, 35, 45
Redemption, 23, 31; and the Diaspora, 93
Reform Judaism, 20, 128; universalism of, 52, 67; opposition to Zionism, 69
Rejuvenation, 74, 79
Renaissance, 38, 39, 41, 59, 72; ch. 3 passim, 91, 98, 108–111; as revival of cultural activity, 73; as adherence to classical culture, 73; as rejuvenation, 74; as revitalization of the past, 75; as re-establishment of Jewish cohesion and independence, 76; and normalization, 77; as awareness of continuity, 83; Jewish cultural, 110
Return, 17, 23, 38–39, 68, 70–72, ch. 1 passim, 54; modern interpretation of, 50; as productivization, 55; and Jewish national aspirations, 61; and territorial and social ingathering, 58; cultural sense of, 61; back to the Land of Israel, 64, 69; Law of Return, 18
Revitalization, 74; giving new momentum to Jewish activity, 77, 78, 79
Ritual, 83, 146
Roman Empire, 47
Rosenzweig, Franz, 128
Rotenstreich, Nathan, *Order and Might*, 114; 1–45 passim, 127–132 passim
Roth, Leon, 2
Russian revolution, 157

S

Scholarship, 1, Jewish excellence in, 112
Scholem, Gershon, 2, "coming back to history," 66
Science, 70, 72, 94, 112, 156, 161, 162
Silver, Abba Hillel, 25
Sinai Campaign, 31
Six-Day War, 29, 35, 36, 123–125; and Messianic expectations, 124
Socialism, 1–45 passim, 65, 72, 130, 160
Society, 1–45 passim, 49, 51, 59, 63, 68; ch.3 passim; Israeli and democracy, 81; and tradition, 82; ch. 5 passim
Solidarity, 12, 29, 35, 38, ch. 5 passim; and economic inequality, 108
Soviet Union, 40, 118, 163
Spain, Muslim, 128
Sparta, Israeli society like, 112
State, 1–45 passim, 59, 61, 69, 70; ch. 2 passim; ch. 3 passim; Israeli, and democracy, 37
Subjugation, 49, 57; and dependence, 49
Supreme Court, Israeli, 114
Survival, 29, 97, 99, 112, 129; and creativity, 97

T

Talmud, 32, and the Bible, 82
Technology, 70, 94, 109, 112, 142
Third Reich, the, 155–164 passim
Tradition, ch. 3 passim

U

Uganda, 57, 60, 70
Universalism, 51; as guiding trend of modern humankind, 51; and return to Land of Israel, 52; support of Reform Judaism for, 67
Universities, 3
Urbach, Ephraim, 83, 85

V

Values, of Israeli society, ch. 5 passim; motivation for adherence to, 102

W

Warsaw, 78
Weizmann, Haim, 159
World War I, 118
World War II, 118
World Zionist Organization, 1–45 passim (also WZO)

Y

Yiddish, 85
Yishuv, the, 1–45 passim, 102–104; as proto state, 102; pioneering spirit of, 103

Z

Zion, 61, 72
Zionism, 1–45 passim; religious precursors of, 51; as national movement, 61; conceptual background of, 62; and modernity, 63; emphasis on Jewish collective existence, 1–45, 64; territorial basis, 68; and nationalism, 68; and "coming back to history," 70; religious Jews opposed to, 69; and territorial/linguistic factors, 70; and return, 71; and revitalization of the past, 74; and return of Hebrew, 74; negative attitude to the Diaspora, 88; Israel as realization of, 101
Zionist Congress, 60
Zionist Labor Movement, 1–45 passim
Zionist, religious, precursors of, 51; distinction between Messiah, Son of David and Messiah, Son of Joseph, 67; rejection of modernity, 69
Zionist, socialist, 1–45 passim; as modernist innovation, 68; and economic, social, moral aspects of Jewish reality, 90, 129